The Person and Ministry of the

HOLY SPIRIT

The Traditional Calvinistic Perspective

The Person and Ministry of the

HOLY SPIRIT

The Traditional Calvinistic Perspective

by Edwin H. Palmer

Baker Book House
Grand Rapids, Michigan

To
my
MOTHER
and
FATHER

Contents

Contents

Introduction

There are few subjects more important to the Christian than the one concerning the Holy Spirit. For the eternal Spirit of God is the source of the Christian's spiritual life: both its origin and continuation. The Holy Spirit is to our spiritual lives what the Creator is to this world. Without God, the Creator, the world would never have come into existence, and without his continuing, sustaining, preserving work, the world would crash out of existence. Similarly, without the Spirit of God, the Christian would never have been born again, and without the Spirit's ever-present sanctifying influence, the spiritual life of the Christian would drop back into the spiritual deadness from which it came. Moreover, a glance at the table of contents of this book will indicate that the Holy Spirit is essential for many other vital aspects of life besides regeneration and sanctification.

Yet in the history of the church the doctrine of the Holy Spirit has often been neglected. Long controversies have centered, for example, around the deity of Christ, the Trinity, grace, atonement, and the sacraments, but shorter controversies around the Holy Spirit. Systematic theologies have dealt with the doctrine of the Spirit in the sections on the Trinity, and briefly in connection with the individual's spiritual life, but have often neglected him in other phases. Christ arouses more enthusiasm than the Holy Spirit; Christmas, than Pentecost. That the Apostles' Creed devotes six articles to Christ and only one to the Spirit is indicative of the proportion of the church's interest. Some have even called the Holy Spirit the "unknown God."

It was the church of the Reformation that gave great impetus to the study of the Spirit. The Reformers, in opposition to Rome's theories, stressed that not the church was necessary for a correct interpretation of the Bible, but rather the Holy Spirit illuminating man's mind. Likewise, in opposing Rome's teaching that the priest was essential in applying to man the unbloody sacrifice of Christ in the mass, Luther and Calvin set forth the necessity of the Holy Spirit in applying the sacrifice of Christ in our lives. But it was chiefly Calvin's rediscovery of the Biblical doctrine of sovereign grace that demanded a heavy emphasis on the doctrine of the Holy Spirit. For Calvin stressed the total depravity of man and unconditional election. This meant, naturally, that if God were to implement his sovereign election, then the Holy Spirit must work powerfully in the lives of the elect.

Perhaps the two most thorough studies on the Holy Spirit are the one written by the English theologian John Owen in the seventeenth century and the volume produced in the last century by the Dutch statesman-theologian Abraham Kuyper, both of whom followed the Reformed heritage. These are, however, so ponderous and detailed that very few take time to read them.

In more recent times there has been an increased tempo in the study of the work of the Spirit. This effort, however, has been directed chiefly towards an analysis of the work of the Spirit in the Christian life—that is, in regeneration and sanctification—to the neglect of the vast work of the Spirit in a range of other matters. With this have also come some aberrations from the Biblical doctrine of the Spirit.

Hence, because of the importance of the subject, its comparative neglect, and the lack of a popular, up-to-date Scriptural study of the Holy Spirit with an emphasis beyond the Christian life, this book has been written.

Edwin H. Palmer

The Holy Spirit and the Trinity 1

In this book we want to consider chiefly the varied work of the Holy Spirit. Before that is possible, however, it is necessary to think about who or what the Holy Spirit is. Hence this initial chapter on the Holy Spirit and the Trinity.

We set forth four propositions concerning this Spirit.

I. The Holy Spirit Is a Person

One of the distinguishing marks of a Christian is his belief in the Holy Spirit as a Person. From the early days of the church to present-day Modernism, there have been those who have denied the personality of the Spirit in one form or another. Many so-called Christian preachers and theologians refer to the Spirit as an "it," and not as a "he." They consider him to be an impersonal influence or power or energy, and not the third Person of the Trinity. Such a view would rob us of some of the great blessings of our salvation. Furthermore, it is not Biblical.

In several ways the Bible reveals to us that the Spirit is a Person. First of all, it attributes to him a mind, will, and emotions, which are exclusively characteristics of a person. Imper-

11

sonal objects do not have these qualities, but the Spirit of God does. Paul presupposes that the Spirit has a mind when he writes that "the Spirit searches all things, even the deep things of God. For who among men knows the thoughts of a man except the man's spirit within him? In the same way no one knows the thoughts of God except the Spirit of God" (I Cor. 2:10, 11).[1] Here Paul ascribes to the Holy Spirit knowledge, which an influence or a power does not have, but a person does. The Bible also pictures the Spirit as possessing the personal quality of a will. We read that when Paul, Silas, and Timothy wanted to go to Bithynia, "the Spirit of Jesus would not allow them to" (Acts 16:7). And in I Corinthians 12:11 Paul tells us that the Spirit gives many gifts to Christians, "just as he determines." As far as emotions are concerned, Ephesians 4:30 assumes that the Spirit can have grief, for it commands us, "Do not grieve the Holy Spirit of God."

A second way in which the Bible reveals that the Spirit is a Person is by placing him in juxtaposition with other persons. For instance, we know that the Father and Son are Persons, and so when Jesus speaks of baptizing disciples "in the name of the Father and of the Son and of the Holy Spirit" (Matt. 28:19), he indicates thereby that the Holy Spirit is a Person, too, just as the Father and the Son are. James, in authorizing certain instructions to the early church, wrote, "It seemed good to the Holy Spirit and to us not to burden you with anything beyond the following requirements" (Acts 15:28). He very clearly considers the Holy Spirit a Person capable of the same thoughts and ideas as he and the apostles had.

Furthermore, it would be a meaningless redundancy to say that Jesus returned from the wilderness "in the power of the Spirit" (Luke 4:14) if the Spirit were simply an impersonal power. Read the phrase again, substituting the word *power* for *Spirit*.

How thankful we must be that the Spirit is a Person! For it is just because he is a Person that he can convict us of sin and thereby lead us to God, dwell within us and give us power over sin, inspire the Bible and illuminate our minds so that we can understand it, guide us so that we know what the will of God is

---

[1] All quotations from the New Testament are taken from the New International Version unless otherwise indicated.

for us, lead us in prayer, and call ministers, elders, and deacons as office-bearers of the church.

Just because the Holy Spirit is a Person we may also react unfavorably toward him. We may resist, grieve, despise, and blaspheme him. This is displeasing to him, and it will surely work harm for ourselves. May we never deny the personality of the Spirit, but believe in him and experience the blessings that can come to us because of this fact.

II. The Holy Spirit Is a Divine Person

Some have believed that the Holy Spirit is a Person, but they have considered him to be a created personality, and not God himself. They have realized that the Spirit is not an impersonal "it," but they have considered him to be inferior to the Father. The Bible, however, attributes to the Holy Spirit not only personal characteristics, but also divine qualities. These divine attributes mark the Holy Spirit as being God.

According to the Scriptures, the Spirit of God is omnipotent, for he has his role in creation (Gen. 1:2), in providence (Ps. 104:30), in the supernatural conception of Jesus (Luke 1:35), in regeneration, and in the equipping of each Christian with spiritual gifts.

He is also omniscient, as Isaiah intimates when he asks: "Who has directed the Spirit of the LORD, or being his counselor has taught him? With whom did he take counsel, and who instructed him and taught him in the path of justice, and taught him knowledge, and showed him the way of understanding?" (40:13, 14). Paul would have us believe the same thing when he writes that "the Spirit searches all things, even the deep things of God" (I Cor. 2:10).

Furthermore, the Holy Spirit may be characterized as being omnipresent. The psalmist eloquently asks: "Where shall I go from your Spirit? Or where shall I flee from your presence?" (Ps. 139:7). He says that he can never escape the Spirit's presence, not even if he ascends to heaven, or descends to Sheol, or flees to the seas, or hides in the blackness of the night. The Spirit is everywhere. In the New Testament we read that the Spirit dwells in believers, and the great number of Christians does not hinder him from being present in each one.

Hebrews 9:14 tells us that Christ "through the eternal Spirit offered himself unblemished to God" thus ascribing to the Holy Spirit the divine quality of eternity.

Another proof of the deity of the Spirit is to be found in the fact that both the Old and New Testaments at times interchange the phrase "the Spirit said" and the phrase "the LORD said."

Lastly, the mere coupling of the name of the Holy Spirit with the names of the Father and the Son, as in the great commission (Matt. 28:19) or in the apostolic benediction (II Cor. 13:14), shows that the Spirit is put on the same level as the other two Persons and, therefore, is considered to be divine. It would be most incongruous to couple the name of a created being with that of the Godhead in such tightly knit expressions.

The fact of the deity of the Holy Spirit is important for us. If he were not God, he could not perform his beautiful work in creation, nor his authoritative work in inspiration, nor his illuminating work in men's minds. Neither could he have overcome our depravity to regenerate, indwell, and sanctify us. We may well be grateful that he is not a finite being but a divine Person.

III. The Holy Spirit Is a Divine Person Distinct from the Father and the Son

In the history of the church there have been those who have believed in the personality of the Holy Spirit and in his deity, but who have so stressed the unity of the Trinity that they have denied that there were three distinct Persons in the Godhead. There were those in the third century who pictured God as appearing in creation as the Father, later on in history as the Son, and finally making his appearance as the Holy Spirit. According to their views there were not simultaneously three Persons in the Godhead. But the one Godhead was called the Father at one time, the Son at another, and the Spirit at a third time. Or the Father first changed into the Son, and later into the Holy Spirit.

These theories, too, are a departure from the revelation of Scripture. Certain Biblical texts are clear in pointing out that there are three distinct Persons and not merely different manifestations of the same God. When Jesus was baptized, for example, the voice of the Father sounded from heaven, saying,

"You are my Son, whom I love; with you I am well-pleased." At the same time, the Spirit descended on Jesus in the form of a dove. The simultaneous appearance of these three Persons makes it impossible to interpret the Godhead simply as a unity. The same may be said of Jesus' statement, *"I* will ask *the Father, and he will give you another Counselor"* (John 14:16). Similarly, Acts 2:33 draws a clear distinction among three Persons of the Godhead: "Exalted to the right hand of God, *he* [i.e., Christ] has received from *the Father* the promised *Holy Spirit.*"

It is a definite blessing to have a God that is not just one Person but three. It makes a rich Trinity. For not only is there a Father who loves us and cares for us, but also a Christ who obtained our salvation and intercedes for us and a Holy Spirit who dwells within us and applies salvation to our lives.

IV. The Holy Spirit Proceeds from the Father and the Son

There is among the three Persons of the Trinity a definite relationship and order. Because the three Persons are equally God, it must not be thought that they are all the same. Each one has distinctive properties and relationships to the others. Between the first and the second Persons, for example, there is the relationship of Father and Son. From all eternity the Father begat the Son. The Holy Spirit did not beget the Son, only the Father did.

In a similar fashion, there is an unchangeable relationship between the Holy Spirit and the other Persons of the Godhead: the Holy Spirit eternally proceeds from the Father and the Son. It is difficult to describe what is meant by the procession of the Spirit of God; we can do little more than repeat the words of Scripture, since the Scriptures do not explain this term. But it is remarkable that the Bible does not say that the Holy Spirit was begotten by the Father, as was Christ, nor that he was begotten by Christ. If that were true, then, as the Church Fathers intimated, the Spirit would have been either a brother to Christ or a grandson to the Father. But the Bible carefully avoids the term *begotten* in relation to the Holy Spirit. As the Athanasian Creed correctly puts it, he was "neither made, nor created, nor begotten, but proceeding." This word *proceed* is used by Jesus in John 15:26, where he says, "When the Counselor comes, whom I will send to you from the Father, the Spirit of truth who proceeds[2] from the Father, he will testify about me."

The name of the Spirit also gives another hint as to this intra-trinitarian relationship. For as the name *Father* shows his relationship to the Son, and the name *Son* describes his relationship to the Father, so also the name *Spirit* points to the relationship of the Spirit to the other two Persons: it is one in which he is *spirated* or breathed, for that is the very meaning of the name *Spirit*.

It must be remembered, however, that although the Spirit proceeds from or is spirated by the Father and the Son, he is still full God. His procession does not mean that he is inferior to the Father or the Son, any more than the generation of the Son means that he is not on an equality with the Father. The secret lies in the fact that the Spirit was *eternally* spirated, just as the Son was *eternally* begotten. There never was a time when the Spirit was not being spirated. He was eternally coexistent with the Father and the Son. To say that he proceeded from or was breathed out by the Father and the Son does not imply that he is less God, but it only indicates the relation that he eternally sustains to the other two Persons of the Trinity.

It should also be noted that the Spirit proceeds from both the Father and the Son, and not only from the Father. That he proceeds from the Father is obvious from John 15:26, but it is not so clear that he also proceeds from the Son. Yet this may be deduced from those passages that tell us that Jesus sends out the Spirit into the world and breathes him onto the disciples (John 15:16; 16:7; 20:22). For the temporal spiration implies an eternal spiration. It reflects a certain authority that the Son has even in the intratrinitarian relationships. Moreover, the Spirit is not only called the "Spirit of the Father," but also the "Spirit of the Son" (Gal. 4:6), the "Spirit of Christ" (Rom. 8:9), and the "Spirit of Jesus Christ" (Phil. 1:19).

This relationship of the Spirit to the other two Persons explains why the Holy Spirit is considered the third Person of the Trinity and not the first or second. The Father is first because

---

[2] For purpose of clarity at this point we have kept the traditional *proceeds* of the King James Version to show the tie-in with the historic theological term of procession, although the New International Version uses the synonym *goes out*.

he begets the Son. The Son is the second Person because he is begotten. The Holy Spirit is third because he proceeds from both the Father and the Son.

It is remarkable that this same order of the Trinity is revealed in history, so that it is not until after the first two Persons have appeared in the foreground in succession that the Holy Spirit comes into prominence. From the time of creation to the time of Christ, it was the Father who was more prominent in the world. He was the one who received the chief glory in creation and with whom Israel in the Old Testament dealt chiefly. When Christ came, the Father did not appear as conspicuously, the Holy Spirit had not yet appeared in his fullness, and Christ played a more prominent role. After the incarnation, however, Christ ascended into heaven, and the third Person of the Trinity appeared on the scene more than the others. Thus because the three Persons have a definite order in the Trinity, that order reveals itself in history, so that each Person appears in history in the same order as he is found in the Trinity itself.

It may also be observed that it was exactly because the Holy Spirit is breathed out by the Father and the Son in the Trinity that it was the Holy Spirit, and not the Father or the Son, who was breathed out on the church at Pentecost. This corresponds to the fact that because the second Person of the Trinity is a Son in the Trinity, he should be the incarnate Son on earth. Similarly, because the first Person of the Trinity is the Father in the Trinity, he is also the Father of believers.

These then are some of the aspects of the relationship of the Holy Spirit to the other two Persons of the Trinity. Although we do not understand very much about this relationship, we should not ignore what the Spirit has revealed but, on the contrary, should rejoice that he has guided his church into a definition of himself and his relationship to the other two Persons, however limited the definition may be. For all of his revelation has a purpose and is not to be disregarded.

As far as the practical results of the doctrine of the spiration of the Spirit of God are concerned, they have been far-reaching. In the year 1054 Christendom was split into the Roman Catholic Church and the Eastern Orthodox Church. Although there were many underlying factors, a stone of stumbling was that the Eastern Christians believed that the Holy Spirit proceeds from the Father alone, whereas the Western churches

confessed with the Council of Toledo (589) that the Spirit proceeds from the Father "and the Son" (*filioque*; that is, *and from
the son,* the term that symbolized the difference). As a result
of these differences, the East separated from the West and today
the Eastern church has a membership of over 160 million. Thus
this doctrine does have enormous practical effects, and if it had
not been formulated by the Church Fathers fifteen hundred
years ago, it could be a burning issue today, affecting our church
lives. Therefore, we must be grateful for the knowledge that
the Holy Spirit has given us on this matter.

Moreover, as Abraham Kuyper has incisively pointed out,
a denial of the *filioque* leads to an unhealthy mysticism. It tends
to isolate the work of the Holy Spirit in our lives from the work
of Jesus. Redemption by Christ is put in the background, while
the sanctifying work of the Spirit is brought to the fore. The
emphasis is more and more on the work of the Spirit in our
lives, which tends to lead to an independence from Christ, the
church, and the Bible. Sanctification can loom larger than justification, the subjective communion with the Spirit larger than
the objective church life, and illumination by the Spirit larger
than the Word. Kuyper believes that this has actually been the
case to some extent in the Eastern church, as a result of the
denial that the Spirit proceeds from the Son as well as from
the Father.

Thus we see that the lengthy theological deliberations that
take place at church councils and synods do at times have a
great influence. Their decisions seep down from the top to
the rank and file, even though the debates do run the risk of
being charged with quibbling. We must be grateful for the
precious revelation that the Holy Spirit has given of his place
in the Trinity, but we should not be satisfied with mere intellectual knowledge. Rather, building upon that, we must strive
to know experientially the Spirit and his workings. To that
end this and the following chapters have been written.

The Holy Spirit and Creation

2

Our study of the Holy Spirit should always remain practical. God's revelation was not intended simply to satisfy our knowledge about the deep things of God, but it was designed to lead us both to glorify God for his greatness and to increase our spiritual growth. Only a clear-cut knowledge of the Holy Spirit in all of his activities will enable us to achieve these purposes. Confusion in our minds as to who the Holy Spirit is or what he does can hinder us from fully glorifying the Spirit and from fully experiencing his varied work in us. Therefore, we now enter upon a study of the *work* of the Spirit.

First of all, it is necessary to guard ourselves against an error. We must not limit the work of the Holy Spirit to that of regeneration and sanctification in the believer. This is done when we consider salvation in the narrow sense to be the most important thing in this world; when we begin and end with man, his sin, his eternal doom, and his need of salvation by Christ. Our view then is chiefly anthropocentric (man-centered), rather than theocentric (God-centered). Our concern then is almost exclusively with salvation, prayer, Bible reading, and matters confined to Sunday and prayer meetings. If we take this point

of view, it is natural to think about the Holy Spirit in terms of
man and his own Christian experience and so in our minds
to restrict the Spirit's activity to that.

This, however, is not the Biblical approach. The Bible begins
with God and not with man. It is theocentric and not anthropocentric. It gives God all the glory and brings him into the
picture from eternity to eternity—including between Sundays.
He is not confined to any one area of life, but is sovereign ruler
over all—absolutely all—in this universe. In harmony with this,
the work of the Holy Spirit may not be restricted exclusively
to sanctification. He had, has, or will have a part in the creation
of this world, in providence, in revelation, in the incarnation,
in redemption, in sanctification, and in events right down to
the day of judgment. That is why in this study we do not restrict our thinking only to the Holy Spirit's work in regeneration or sanctification; for this is not a discussion of the work
of the Holy Spirit in sanctification alone, but of the entire work
of the Holy Spirit.

I. The Work of the Trinity in Creation

In this world there are special functions and works performed
by each Person of the Trinity in distinction from the other two.
When we think of creation, for example, we think chiefly of
the Father, and not of the Son or the Holy Spirit. On the
cross, however, it was Christ who died, and not the Father, nor
the Holy Spirit. Jesus even distinguished himself from the
Father on the cross, when he cried out, "My God, my God, why
have you forsaken me?" and "Father, into your hands I commit
my spirit." And when we think of sanctification and the working out of salvation in our lives, we do not think chiefly of the
Father, nor the Son, but of the Holy Spirit. He is the one who
dwells within the Christian. In fact, it is because of the neglect
of these distinctions that some people who are in anxiety and
distress go to the Father or Christ for comfort, when, in reality,
they should go to the Holy Spirit, who is *the* Holy Comforter.

Yet, at the same time, there is a sense in which we may not
separate the three Persons. Although we do think of the Father
chiefly as the Creator, yet because of the basic, essential unity
in the Trinity, it may also be said that the Son and the Holy
Spirit created. Although it is self-evident that it was the Son

who died on the cross, yet in a certain sense the Father was there, too, for Jesus coud say, "I and the Father are one." And although it is perfectly Biblical to assert that it is the Holy Spirit who dwells in our hearts, yet Christ could say of the Christian, ". . . my Father will love him, and we will come to him, and make our home with him" (John 14:23). And Paul could assert, "Christ lives in me" (Gal. 2:20). These things can be true for the simple reason that within the Trinity, even though there are distinct Persons, there is also a basic unity, for the three are one.

In our thinking on this matter, and especially as it pertains to the subject of creation, we must always keep before us this perfect balance, even if we cannot understand it entirely: the balance, on the one hand, of the diversity of the Trinity and of their work in this world, and, on the other hand, of the basic unity among the three. We may not separate them as if one of them can act all alone without the others, and yet we may, following the Bible, ascribe to one, in distinction from the other two, certain characteristics and work.

In general, the Scriptures indicate that the work of the Trinity is from the Father, through the Son, and to the Holy Spirit. The Father originates, the Son executes, and the Holy Spirit perfects. In redemption, for example, it is the Father who loved the world so much "that he gave his one and only Son" (John 3:16). Ephesians 1:3 tells us that it was the "Father of our Lord Jesus Christ" who loved the elect and foreordained them unto adoption in Christ Jesus. The Bible ascribes the electing love as being "from the Father," and not from the Son nor the Holy Spirit. And it was the Son who accomplished that redemption in time. It was not the Father nor the Holy Spirit who came into the world, but the Son. Thus redemption is "through the Son." Likewise, it is the Holy Spirit who applies this redemption to the life of the Christian and brings redemption to its completion. Redemption is "to the Holy Spirit." Thus the work of redemption may be said to be "from the Father, through the Son, and to the Holy Spirit."

The same distinctions that are found in redemption are to be found also in creation. The created universe is also from the Father, through the Son, and to the Holy Spirit. The Bible indicates that each Person in the Trinity did not perform the same function in creation. Rather, "there is but one God, the

Father, of whom are all things, . . . and one Lord Jesus Christ, through whom are all things" (I Cor. 8:6). Notice that all things are "from" the Father, but "through" the Son. The indication is that the Father is the source of all things and that the Son is the one who, using these materials, then constructed the world. Romans 11:36 speaks in a similar fashion when it uses three different prepositions in the statement: "For *from* him and *through* him and *to* him are all things." Hebrews 1:1, 2 speaks in the same vein when it says that "God has spoken to us by his Son . . . *through* whom he made the universe." John 1 and Colossians 1 also mention that the world was created "through" the Son and "by him." Elsewhere, as we shall see presently, the Bible speaks of the Holy Spirit as perfecting the work of the Father and the Son.

Abraham Kuyper, in his work *The Holy Spirit,* illustrated this by comparing the creation of the universe to the building of a king's palace. The king supplies the materials for the palace, but the contractor does the actual building. So in creation, the Father, as the king, is the source from whom all things were created out of nothing. The Son is like the contractor who, taking the materials furnished, constructed the universe. The Holy Spirit is the one who added to what the Son accomplished and completed it, drawing out the potentialities and causing it to develop according to its nature.

In all of this, however, as we have seen, we must remember the underlying unity of all the Persons of the Trinity and not separate their activity, so that in a certain sense all three Persons are simultaneously active in both redemption and creation. To understand this perfectly is impossible. It is a mystery. Yet we may attempt to understand and to describe the Trinity's work insofar as the Biblical revelation allows it.

II. The Work of the Holy Spirit in Creation

With these trinitarian distinctions as a background for our thinking, we may now proceed to see what the Bible says more directly about the work of the Holy Spirit in creation. There are at least five distinct aspects of this work that can be mentioned.

A. When we turn to the story of creation in Genesis 1, we notice that the work of the Spirit is not that of creating the materials of the world out of nothing, but that his work comes after that. In Genesis 1:1, 2 we read: "In the beginning God created the heavens and the earth. And the earth was waste and void; and darkness was upon the face of the deep." Only after that, after there was a creation of the universe out of nothing, does the Bible mention the activity of the Spirit by saying, "and the Spirit of God moved upon the face of the waters." The implication is that the Father, who even within the Trinity is the "source and fountain" of the Son and the Holy Spirit, is also the source and fountain of the material universe, creating it out of nothing; and that after that was accomplished, the Holy Spirit moved upon the face of the waters, bringing a certain order out of what had already been made. He did not create the world, but he drew out potentialities that were already in the world, and even implanted the seeds and germs of life, as we shall see presently.

B. Psalm 33:6 and Job 26:13 give another indication of the perfecting work of the Holy Spirit, this time in the embellishing of the heavens. The psalmist tells us in 33:6 that "by the word of the LORD were the heavens made, and all the host of them by the breath of his mouth." As we saw in the first chapter, *Spirit* means *breath,* and the Holy Spirit is breathed out by the Father and the Son. Therefore it is justifiable to translate *breath* by *Spirit* in this psalm. The meaning would be that the LORD created the heavens, and the Spirit was active in the production of the hosts of heaven—the stars, planets, moon, and sun. Job 26:13 does not necessarily indicate that the Spirit created the hosts, but he did cause them to be beautiful, for Job says: "By his Spirit the heavens are garnished." *To garnish* means "to make fair or glorious or beautiful." Thus Job tells us that the Spirit took the heavens that were already created by God and caused them to be as beautiful as we see them now, with the constellations, the Milky Way, the planets reflecting the light of the sun, the different colors of the stars, the largeness of the moon and the steadiness of its light, and the brilliance of the sun. In other words, just as Genesis 1:2 indicates that the Spirit perfected the world that had been created, so here the implication is that the Holy Spirit put on the finishing touches in the heavens, drawing out the glory and beauty that were possible in the hosts of heaven.

C. Psalm 104 tells us of another aspect of the creative activity of the Holy Spirit: the giving of life to birds, fish, and animals.

This beautiful psalm of the providence of God ascribes all the phenomena of nature to God, declaring that God is the One who controls all things, and that all things depend upon him. The wild donkeys quench their thirst from the springs that God makes, the cattle eat from the grass that God causes to grow, the birds make nests in the cedars of Lebanon that God plants, the roaring lion seeks its food from God, and even the leviathan in the sea waits upon God for its sustenance. All beasts and living creatures, great and small, depend upon him for their existence. Says the psalmist in verse 29, "You hide your face, they are troubled; you take away their breath, they die and return to dust." But it is also God, and more specifically the Holy Spirit, who gives life; for the psalmist continues in verse 30, "You send forth your Spirit, they are created; and you renew the face of the ground." Thus the psalmist indicates that the Holy Spirit is the one who gives life to all living creatures: to the storks in the fir trees, the wild goats in the mountains, and the leviathans in the great seas—to bird, beast, and fish.

Thus Scripture leads us to consider the creative activity of the Holy Spirit, not in the direction of making something out of nothing, but in imparting life to that which has already been created, in line with what we discovered in Genesis 1 and Job 26:13.

D. This same Psalm 104 also gives hints that even vegetation receives its life from the Spirit. The verse which we just quoted says, "You send forth your Spirit, they are created; and you renew the face of the ground." The latter part of this verse does not explicitly mention the Holy Spirit as the one who renews the ground. Yet since it is closely connected with the first part of the verse (where the Holy Spirit is mentioned), since he gives life to animals as well as men (as we will presently see), and since in general his work is not that of an originator but of a perfecter, it seems safe to infer that it is the Spirit who also renews the ground. The meaning, then, of this verse is that although there is in all of creation after the fall of man the seed of death—so that vegetation, animals, and man all die eventually—yet it is by the constant creative activity of the Holy Spirit that this decaying, dying process is checked, and life is given instead. He not only gives life to the birds, fish, and beasts, but he renews the earth by causing the grass, plants, and trees to grow. Seeds containing life are

produced, which in their season will grow. After the deadness
of winter, new life comes forth and the ground is renewed.
Hence even vegetational life, both at the time of creation and
today, is produced by the Holy Spirit.

E. The climax of the creative work of the Spirit was and is
the creation of man. Elihu's words are very clear when he says,
"The Spirit of God has made me, and the breath of the Almighty gives me life" (Job 33:4). *Breath,* of course, being another name for *Spirit,* this verse names the Holy Spirit twice in
the creation of man. The specific creative function of the Spirit
seems to be the giving of life, indicating again that he did not
necessarily create matter, but, taking the dust of the earth, he
breathed into it the breath of life.

It is interesting to notice that the creation account of man in
Genesis 2:7 describes the making of man by the words "God . . .
breathed into his nostrils the breath of life," using the words
breathed and *breath,* the latter being the name of the Holy
Spirit, and the former containing it. From Job 33:4, which
states clearly that it is the third Person of the Trinity that gives
life to man, we may infer that Genesis 2:7 gives us a definite
suggestion, too, that it was the Holy Spirit, rather than the Father
or the Son, who gave and gives life to man.

It is, then, the Holy Spirit who is responsible for the creating
of man as a man. Man became a *living soul,* and not just a moving animal. The Holy Spirit gave to man his rational and moral
being. He is the one who made man so that he has a mind, will,
and emotions. Job 32:8 confirms this in part when it says, "But
there is a spirit in man, and the breath [Spirit] of the Almighty
gives them understanding." And it is also the Holy Spirit who
made man good, upright, holy, and righteous.

These, then, are five distinguishing characteristics of the creative work of the Holy Spirit. Although we must be on our guard
against doing violence to the unity of the three Persons of the
Trinity, yet we may and must ascribe to each Person the particular functions that the Bible ascribes to him. When, on a cold
winter's night, we see in the blackness of the sky the ever-familiar
Great Dipper; or bright Orion, the mighty hunter; or the faint
Pleiades; or the red wanderer, Mars; or the Northern Cross; or
the nebulous swath, the Milky Way, let us praise the Holy Spirit
for having garnished the heavens. When in spring we see the
wheat seeds sprouting, the violets blooming, and the dogwood

blossoming, let us remember that it is the Spirit who renews the face of the ground. When we catch perch, see a deer leap across a field, and follow the flight of a red-headed woodpecker, remember Psalm 104:29, 30: "You take away their breath, they die and return to dust. You send forth your Spirit, they are created." When, as a proud mother and father, we hear with excitement the first cry of our baby, recall to mind the words of Elihu, who said, "The Spirit of God has made me, and the breath [Spirit] of the Almighty gives me life." These are the results of the creative activity of the Holy Spirit, and for these things we must give him the glory.

III. The Work of the Holy Spirit in Re-creation

There is one final creative activity of the Holy Spirit that should be mentioned, and that is his re-creative work in regeneration and sanctification. This will be dealt with more fully in later chapters but should be touched on here in order to give a complete picture of the Spirit's work in creation. After the Spirit had breathed into man the breath of life, giving unto him righteousness, holiness, and knowledge, man fell from his original high estate of rectitude. He became marred, scarred, bruised, mangled, and even dead spiritually. He lost his true knowledge and his holy disposition. He ceased to be what the Spirit had made him.

But our good God did not leave man in such a grievous state. Rather, by means of the One who made man righteous and holy in the first place, the Holy Spirit, he re-created man. The Holy Spirit made him a new creation in Christ (II Cor. 5:17). He made man his "workmanship, created in Christ Jesus to do good works" (Eph. 2:10). He caused him to be renewed by implanting in him a new man that has been "created to be like God in true righteousness and holiness" (Eph. 4:24; Col. 3:10).

Notice the similarity between the first creation and this re-creation of man by the Holy Spirit. The Holy Spirit gave to Adam a righteousness that was spotless. So, also, in re-creation the Holy Spirit makes it possible for man to have the righteousness of Jesus Christ that is perfect. This is an even better righteousness than Adam's, since this can never be lost, whereas Adam's not only could be, but was lost.

Also, as in the first creation the Holy Spirit made man person-

ally holy, so in the second creation the Spirit makes man personally holy by regeneration and sanctification.

Next notice that as in the creation of the world the Holy Spirit
did not create out of nothing, but gave life, order, and beauty to
a dead, inert, dark earth that was waste and void by "brooding
over the face of the waters," so also in the new creature in Christ,
there is not a destruction of sinful man and then a creating of a
new man out of nothing. The Holy Spirit does not create an
entirely new man, but, as in the first creation, taking that which
is already existent, which has become dead in sins and trespasses
(Eph. 2:1), he imparts spiritual life in Christ Jesus, giving to
man new dispositions so that he can become as he was at the
first creation—holy, righteous, and full of truth.

Finally, as in creation man became a living soul by the breathing of life into man, so also in the re-creation, the Holy Spirit
is breathed out upon the church of Christ so that man becomes
spiritually alive.

The creative work of the Holy Spirit, then, is all-embracing,
pertaining both to the physical and spiritual realms. It began
in a special way at creation. It continues throughout today, including even the re-creation of man. The aim of this book is
that we all may know the Holy Spirit as Creator, either for the
first time or as he is ever anew creating righteousness and holiness within us.

The Holy Spirit and Common Grace

3

One of the least recognized, but one of the most far-reaching, activities of the Holy Spirit is his work in common grace. This consists of his restraining the reprobate from doing evil, his encouragement of the reprobate to do good, and the instilling in the reprobate of certain abilities to perform cultural tasks.

I. The Problem

To understand more fully the work of the Holy Spirit in common grace, it is necessary to observe the background which made common grace necessary. When the Holy Spirit made man, he made him perfect. He breathed into him the breath of life, and man became a living soul made in the image of the Creator. Being the *Holy* Spirit, he endowed him with holiness, righteousness, and knowledge: there was no evil in him at all.

After Adam fell, he, and all of mankind with him, was no longer in his original state of moral uprightness. On the contrary, his nature was now depraved. Scripture tells us that man's nature became *totally* depraved. That means that it was wholly inclined to evil and to no spiritual good whatsoever.

29

The natural man,[1] that is, the man without the supernatural working of the Holy Spirit in his life, does not in the basic sense know God nor truth. Although he seems to understand many things, he does not understand a single thing truly because he does not relate it to the God of the Bible. He should be able to know God by observing God's power and wisdom in the works of nature, but Romans 1:18 tells us that the natural man suppresses this truth, hinders it, holds it down in unrighteousness. In I Corinthians 2:14, 15, we read that "the man without the Spirit [or *the natural man,* KJV] does not accept the things that come from the Spirit of God, for they are foolishness to him, and he cannot understand them, because they are spiritually discerned."

Not only does natural man not know the things about God, but he hates God and has involved himself in such a moral predicament by his willful disobedience that he is no longer able to do one single thing that is spiritually good in God's sight. This may seem hard to believe and very harsh language. Yet, if we believe the Bible to be God's infallible Word, we must admit that it is so.

The Scriptures tell us that the imagination of the thoughts of the heart of man is continuously evil, from his youth up (Gen. 6:5; 8:21). Jeremiah (17:9) says that "the heart is deceitful above all things, and desperately wicked. Who can know it?" Paul says in unmistakable tones: "There is no one righteous, not even one; there is no one who understands, no one who searches for God. All have turned away and together become worthless. There is no one who does good, not even one. Their throats are open graves; their tongues practice deceit. The poison of vipers is on their lips. Their mouths are full of cursing and bitterness. Their feet are swift to shed blood; ruin and misery mark their paths, and the way of peace they do not know. There is no fear of God before their eyes" (Rom. 3:10-18). In another place he adds: "The sinful mind is hostile to God. It does not submit to God's law, nor can it do so. Those controlled by their sinful nature cannot please God" (Rom. 8:7, 8). And in Ephesians Paul says that man is dead in sins and trespasses—not sick, not injured, but dead to all good works (2:1).

Thus the Christian church has confessed that, although the

---

[1] The term "natural man" is taken from the King James Version, where it is often used for man in his natural state, untouched by the Holy Spirit.

Holy Spirit created Adam holy and upright, yet, because of his sin, man's nature was corrupted, so that nothing but evil proceeds from him. And if left to his wicked ways and inclinations, he will follow them to the hilt, giving outward expression to his inward wickedness, as was the case of those whom God gave up to a reprobate mind (Rom. 1:26 ff.).

This, then, is the natural condition of man. Yet, and this is the problem, natural man is not as evil as he could be. Natural man does many things that are outwardly noble and pleasing. The unregenerate has not entirely followed his evil inclinations. There are those who, not being Christian, and even knowing the gospel of Christ and yet willfully rejecting it, in some ways outshine the Bible-believing, church-going Christian. At times their tempers are more even, their lusts are more subdued, their generosity is greater, their truthfulness is more spontaneous, their children do not cheat, as do the children of many Christians, they are more considerate of the feelings of others, and their integrity is of the highest order. In other words they are "splendid" people, even if they are not Christians.

The problem which has confronted the Christian church in times past has been: How do you explain this? If man, according to the Bible, is *totally* depraved, if there is no goodness within him whatsoever, if he does not have an iota of ability to do or even desire to do a single thing that is good, if he is inclined to hate God and his neighbor, how, then, is it possible that he can do this apparent "good," be a "splendid" pagan, and live a life that seems at times to be even better than the lives of Christians?

The tendency of some is to deny the evil in man. They point to non-Christians of apparently virtuous character. They say that man is inwardly really good and not so evil after all; that he is like a rock that is rough and dirty-looking on the outside, but when broken open is found to contain beautiful gems on the inside. And so inwardly, man is good, even though sometimes he appears bad outwardly.

Yet this solution must be firmly rejected if we believe the Bible. For as we have seen, the Biblical facts are just the opposite. Eternally lost, man is outwardly beautiful at times but inwardly rotten to the core. He is like a highly polished, red, juicy-looking, tight-skinned apple that some child might delight in, but when that child takes a bite, his teeth sink into a pulpy, rotten core, crawling with worms, which he immediately spits out or gags on.

And the solution may not be found in the fact that the Holy Spirit is working within him in a saving way, for that is exactly what we are not talking about. We are not speaking of the Christian, but of the reprobate, the one who never was born again and never will be, the one who will spend eternity in hell.

II. The Solution

The answer that the Bible gives to this problem is that the Holy Spirit works in the lives of non-Christians in a special way. He does not work in a saving way. It is not regeneration. It is not through the process of sanctification. But outside of the Christian, the Holy Spirit does work in a certain way in those who are the reprobate, who are the nonelect. This is called *common grace.*

It is *grace* because they do not deserve this working of the Holy Spirit a bit. What they deserve is the sentence of Romans 1:18 and following, which speaks of God leaving them alone and allowing them to become hardened in their unbelief and wickedness. They deserve nothing but condemnation and punishment. What they receive is unmerited favor. Therefore it is called *grace.*

This grace is popularly called *common* because it is generally regarded as not only for the elect—for God's people, for Christians—but for the nonelect, too. It is considered common to both the saved and the unsaved.

Strictly speaking, however, this is not accurate terminology. For this grace is *not* common to both the unregenerate and the regenerate. There are two entirely different types of grace. The saving, sin-restraining operation of the Holy Spirit in the lives of the elect is the result of special grace—of God's special, electing love for his chosen ones. The nonsaving, sin-restraining working of the Holy Spirit in the lives of the reprobate is the result of common grace—of God's love for the nonelect. The restraint is common to both, but the grace—the love that causes the restraint—differs.

Be that as it may, "common grace" also includes other matters than the working of the Spirit in people's lives. It includes the fact that God sincerely offers salvation to those who are lost, even though they are not elected and never will believe. It includes many things of the providence of this world, such as the giving of sunshine and rain to unbelievers, the maintenance of the laws of nature so that crops can grow, and the granting of healing powers to a sick body. It also means that God is longsuffering in the execution of his punishment upon unbelievers, not meting out immediately their just deserts.

But common grace also includes a general operation of the Holy Spirit in the nonelect, and it is this aspect with which we want to deal in this chapter, and not with common grace in general. This work of the Spirit is threefold. There is a negative aspect, the restraining of sin in the lives of individuals; and a positive one, the encouragement to do good, even if it is not good done out of faith. In addition, there is a third aspect, the endowing of natural man with general abilities so that he can perform certain cultural tasks. We must now examine this threefold operation of the Holy Spirit further to see how far-reaching its effects are.

A. *Restraint from Sin.* First of all, Scripture indicates that God sends his Holy Spirit among the nonelect to restrain them from following their evil inclinations to the utmost. This in no way renders their deeds pleasing in God's sight but simply makes them less wicked. It means that life in this world is tolerable and livable because men have been prevented by the Holy Spirit from going to excesses.

God may check the evil in men's lives in many ways. He may do it by acts of providence. He may bridle sexual immorality by having it often accompanied by venereal diseases, so that people themselves will curb their lustful desires because of fear of consequences. Or he may thwart evil intentions by causing a flood to wipe out all or some of the inhabitants, as in Noah's day. But also, and this is the point we are interested in now, God restrains evil by a direct working of the Holy Spirit on the souls of individuals, not in a saving way, but nevertheless so that those individuals are bridled in their disobedience to God.

Saul, for example, was probably not saved, yet the Spirit of the LORD was in his life, causing him to do good. But after a period of disobedience, "the Spirit of the LORD departed from Saul, and an evil spirit from the LORD troubled him" (I Sam. 16:14).

Isaiah complained of the wickedness of Israel. He writes that "they rebelled, and grieved his holy Spirit: therefore he turned to be their enemy and fought against them" (Isa. 63:10). In other words, it was the Holy Spirit who was in the lives of many Israelites in a nonsaving way, restraining sin in their lives, even though later on their wickedness caused the Spirit to be withdrawn from them and even to fight against them.

Stephen spoke in a similar vein when he told the Jews of their rebellious acts from the days of Abraham to the murdering of Christ. He then sharply rebuked them: "You stubborn people, with uncircumcised hearts and ears! You are just like your fathers: You always resist the Holy Spirit!" (Acts 7:51). To say that they resisted the Spirit implies that the Spirit had been working in their hearts in some way, even though they were unregenerated.

And of course the Epistle to the Hebrews mentions the working of the Holy Spirit in the lives of non-Christians to the extent that they were "enlightened," "tasted the heavenly gift," and "shared in the Holy Spirit" (Heb. 6:4). Yet after they committed the unpardonable sin, the Spirit withdrew from their lives never to work a work of repentance in them. Being lost for eternity, those reprobate had nevertheless had the Holy Spirit in their lives in a nonsaving way.

Thus the Holy Spirit works in the lives of nonbelievers, restraining them from evil. How grateful we may be to God that through his common grace he gives his Holy Spirit to those who are lost, to those who are damned eternally. For without this grace men would go to excess; they would give full rein to their sinful desires. Life would become intolerable. There would be more sadism, more robbery, more drunkenness, more immorality. Divorce would be even more rampant. Violence would be the order of the day. It would be unsafe to walk down the street. The whole community and nation would be saturated with every form of sin. For there are times, according to Scripture, when God no longer strives with man, but abandons him to his own wicked pleasures. The greater the abandonment, the more intolerable life becomes.

God, speaking through Asaph, mentioned this withdrawal of the Holy Spirit when he said: "But my people did not listen to my voice, and Israel would have none of me. So I gave them over to the stubbornness of their hearts, that they might walk according to their own counsels" (Ps. 81:11, 12). Stephen declared that God gave the Israelites up to serve the host of heaven. Isaiah said that the Holy Spirit even fought against the Israelites. Paul emphasizes the lusts, deceits, hates, perversions, strife, insolence, and invention of new evils that were the lot of those whom God abandoned (Rom. 1).

In II Thessalonians we have a description of what will happen in the end of this age when the Holy Spirit is removed from the world. For, says Paul, "the secret power of lawlessness is already at work; but the one [i.e., the Holy Spirit] who now holds it back will continue to do so till he is taken out of the way" (2:7). The spirit of the Antichrist, who is already present in the world, is being restrained. One day, however, that restraint will be removed. Then will come the end, and the Antichrist will be revealed, that "man of lawlessness," "the man doomed to destruction," who "opposes and exalts himself over everything that is called God or is worshiped, and even sets himself up in God's temple, proclaiming himself to be God" (2:4). Then there will be persecutions, and the Antichrist will come in all of his horribleness against Christ and Christians, following the dictates of his wanton wishes, performing great acts of unrestrained violence and wickedness. This is what will happen when the restraint of sin is removed, when the Holy Spirit withdraws his influence and delivers man up to his own desires. The world will then be an intolerable place in which to live. And all of this would occur now if the One who restrains were removed today.

Thus one of the most stupendous workings of the Holy Spirit today is among the reprobate, deterring them from their evil ways and making life livable. For we Christians are in the minority in this world. We represent only a very small percentage of the population. Were it not for this restraining work of the Spirit, life would be unbearable for the Christian. And the Christian may well pray to the Holy Spirit that he will work increasingly in the lives of the unregenerate that we may have a world of peace and tranquility where we can live without fear.

B. *Encouragement to Good.* A second major work of the Holy Spirit in the sphere of common grace is the reverse of the previously mentioned work. The very restraint from sin means that man must do something relatively good. There can be no vacuum. If something is taken away, something else must take its place. Or, in another figure of speech, the removal of some

black from an object means that the object must necessarily, in
the nature of the case, become a little grayer. So it is in the
spiritual realm. As the Holy Spirit works in unregenerated man,
two things happen: man is restrained from evil, and he is en-
couraged to do good. In spite of his totally corrupt nature, by
the grace of the Holy Spirit unregenerate man does things that
are formally and outwardly pleasing to God.

It should be clearly remembered, however, that the natural
man does absolutely nothing that is truly pleasing before God,
since he lacks faith, and "everything that does not come from
faith is sin" (Rom. 14:23). He can do things which outwardly
conform to the law of God, but because he does not love Jesus
Christ, because he does not honor God, and because he does not
do these things out of a pure motive of love and faith toward
God, every action of the unregenerate man is sin.

To make absolutely clear what the Bible teaches—if a Unitarian, who denies the deity of Jesus Christ and who relies on
himself instead of on Jesus to save him, should give a million
dollars for the missionary work of a church that preaches Jesus
Christ crucified and risen for sinners, that giving would not be,
on the giver's part, an act of spiritual good. For it would not be
done out of faith in Christ and to his glory, but for another
reason. Although, to be sure, such an action would be far better
than if that amount were spent on prostitution or gambling, yet
without the proper motive, no act is fundamentally pleasing to
God. That is what we mean by saying it is *relatively* good, but
not *truly* good.[2]

That the Spirit of God does encourage the reprobate to a
relative good is seen from some Scriptural examples. The Old
Testament mentions three kings, for example, Jehu, Jehoash,
and Amaziah, who did not truly fear God, who were reprobate.
Yet of Jehu God says in the Bible: "Because you have done well
in executing what is right in my eyes . . . your sons of the fourth
generation will sit on Israel's throne" (II Kings 10:30). Of

[2] These terms, *relatively good* and *truly good,* could be misleading. For
in a sense, even the regenerate's deeds are not *truly* good, since nothing he
does is perfect. Yet, the title of Article XIV of the Belgic Confession, without using the expression *relatively good,* speaks of the *truly good.* Neither
is it accurate to speak of *saving good,* since the Christian is not saved by
good works, but by Christ. The distinction we make is also described by
some with the terms *civic good* and *spiritual good.*

Jehoash the Bible says that he "did that which was right in the eyes of the LORD" (II Kings 12:2). And the writer repeats the same words for King Amaziah. Thus these kings did things that were pleasing before God, even though they themselves were ultimately lost.

In the New Testament the fact that the reprobate do good is expressly stated by Christ when he commanded the disciples to love not only their friends, but also their enemies, for he reasoned: "And if you do good to those who are good to you, what credit is that to you? Even 'sinners' do that" (Luke 6:33). In other words, Christ says that the nonelect do good. Again, this may not be taken to mean that they do that which is *truly* good, but that they perform a *relative* good.

And Paul writes to the Romans (2:14) that the "Gentiles, who do not have the law, do by nature things required by the law." They do not know Jesus Christ, they do not have the revelation we have, and yet they that are the reprobate do things which are outwardly in accordance with the law of God, things which are pleasing to God in a relative sense.

Even today the Holy Spirit moves people to do things which are outwardly in conformity with the law of God. It is because of the Holy Spirit that wealthy unbelievers give money to schools and hospitals, instead of spending it on luxuries; that a Christ-denying Unitarian will help a little two-year-old, who has fallen off his tricycle, to set the bike straight again, and will take the little boy on his knee, wiping away the tears and trying to distract him from his fall; that a blasphemer will give money to a beggar; that a Jew will give a hundred dollars for the relief of tornado victims; that a godless American soldier will show mercy on an enemy; that a Bible-ridiculing politician will strive for peace; and that a boastful pagan will willingly sacrifice his life to rescue a drowning boy.

These and other deeds by the unregenerate are due to the nonsaving operations of the Holy Spirit in their lives. And we may well thank God for this wonderful grace which makes life so pleasant and livable. We may also look with shame upon ourselves who profess Christianity and yet are filled with so much bickering, jealousy, backbiting, lust, and hate; while others who do not know Christ as their personal Savior live outwardly, at least, lives that are often better than ours. May God deliver us from our inconsistency. But at the same time, let us praise

God for this second work of the Holy Spirit in the reprobate, whereby life is made not only bearable but so enjoyable.

C. *The Endowment for Cultural Tasks.* A third sphere of the Holy Spirit's influence in common grace is to be found in his endowing the non-Christian with intellectual capacities, mechanical skills, artistic ability, and capabilities in science, languages, music, and general culture. The regenerate have no monopoly on these matters. It is only too evident that just exactly those who are not Christian are often more skilled and accomplished than the Christian.

This endowment by the Holy Spirit follows from the fact, as we saw in the last chapter, that it is the Spirit who breathes into man the breath of life and who is therefore the origin of the soul, the mind, and the faculties of reason and emotions. This breath of life, this soul, this understanding that the Spirit gives to man is also the source of cultural achievements. In Isaiah 45:1 we read that the heathen King Cyrus was anointed by God to do his work. The Spirit was sent to Cyrus to give him wisdom, courage, and military skill so that he could perform the task God had for him. Undoubtedly that same non-regenerative activity of the Holy Spirit continues today.

It is because the Spirit endowed natural man with great faculties that Aristotle could gain such a tremendously broad knowledge, Caesar could conquer and rule so many lands, the ancient Greeks could devise such lasting architecture, Shakespeare could write such enduring plays as *Macbeth* and *Hamlet,* Beethoven could compose his *Fifth Symphony,* Einstein could formulate the theory of relativity. These are the gifts of the Holy Spirit. May we thank God for them, and may we use them to his glory.

Hence there is a threefold work of the Holy Spirit, in distinction from that of the Father and the Son, in the field of common grace. He restrains the unregenerate from sin, incites him to good, and qualifies him to great cultural attainments. These are the things that make this world livable and beautiful. The effects are stupendous, and Hodge was correct when he said that "the greatest calamity that can befall an individual, a church, or a people, is that God should take his Holy Spirit from them."

Conclusion

In closing, a word of warning is in order. Although we know

that the Holy Spirit works in the lives of the reprobate, we must not think for a moment that this saves a person. These operations of the Holy Spirit are not saving operations. They save no one. Salvation comes only by trusting in Jesus Christ as one's own Savior. That trust is also worked by the Holy Spirit. And it is only when the Spirit operates in that fashion, causing a person to commit his life to Christ, that he is saved.

Some might think that since the Holy Spirit works within them to enable them to become clever with their hands or to run a business, and because the Spirit has restrained them from sin and has even incited them to do some things that are outwardly rather good, they will be saved. But this is not Biblical. The Bible says nowhere that a person who does good shall be saved. We must recognize that the Holy Spirit works in the unbeliever and unregenerate to do good, and we must be thankful to God for this tremendous, far-reaching influence of his Spirit. But the simple fact is that this influence and working of the Holy Spirit will carry no one to heaven. The sinner needs not only common grace; he needs special grace in order to be saved. He needs faith in Jesus Christ, the Son of God. He that calls upon the name of the Lord shall be saved. He that believes on the only begotten Son shall have eternal life. So, be thankful for the work of the Holy Spirit in common grace, but let not a single person be deceived into thinking that he is saved by it. Rather, let him see that salvation belongs only to those who confess their sins, renounce their old ways, and ask Jesus to redeem them.

The Holy Spirit and Revelation 4

In this study on the Holy Spirit we are dealing with tremendous themes. We have seen some of the eternal mysteries of the Godhead, such as the processional relationship of the Holy Spirit to the Father and to the Son, the perfecting role that the Holy Spirit played in the creation of this world, and the momentous effects of the Holy Spirit in common grace. In the chapters to follow we will deal with other important themes, such as the role of the Holy Spirit in incarnation, regeneration, sanctification, and the church.

In this present chapter we come to still another great work of the Holy Spirit, his work in revelation. By revelation we mean that act of God by which he makes known to man certain things that were hidden and unknown. That occurs in two ways: through nature and through the Bible.

I. The Problem of Knowledge

Divine revelation is of the utmost importance because it is the source of all our knowledge. Throughout the ages men—Christians and non-Christians alike—have been interested in knowledge. They want to know the truth about themselves, about nature, and about God. They have a basic craving within their natures to know and to know with certainty. Only by revelation does man gain true knowledge of anything. By revelation God makes himself known to men and also reveals the true nature of things in the world, whether of men or of natural objects.

The non-Christian denies, explicitly or implicitly, God's revelation, and therefore he is groping without success for the truth. He denies the Christian God and hence he denies the only possible way of knowing things truly—by revelation. He lacks absolute certainty in knowledge. He guesses and says "perhaps" and "maybe" and "I think," but he never knows with finality. But when one goes to the God of the Bible and to his revelation, he has the basis for true knowledge. For God, by his revelation, tells man many things. God tells something about his likes and dislikes, his foreordained plans, the rule of life by which man must walk, the way of salvation, the reality and nature of this world, certain laws, and what will 'happen after death, to name only a few. Man may know with absolute certainty things that could never have been known otherwise, things concerning both this created world and God. The man who learns through God's revelation has a firm foundation which is eternally unmovable. His knowledge will not shift with time. This gives him an overwhelming satisfaction. He has something which the philosophers —and every man is a philosopher at heart—have sought for since the day of Adam.

This divine revelation is twofold. It is a natural revelation and a supernatural revelation; or, better still, a general revelation and a special revelation. That first revelation, general revelation, is to be found wherever you are. It is in the flowers in your garden, in the television set in your living room, in the raindrops on the window pane, in the leaves on the trees, in the blade of grass, in a child's finger. In fact, it is in any and all things that are created. All things were made by God, and they reveal in themselves something of God, show something of his glory, power, wisdom, and Godhead. You do not have to see God with your physical eye to know him.

It is possible to know some of God's characteristics by observing nature. "The heavens," says David, "declare the glory of God" (Ps. 19:1). It is almost as if the sun, the moon, and the stars could talk, so clear are the things of God that they reveal, such as his infinity and omnipotence. When man examines the moonbeams, or the brilliance of the sun, or sees the millions of stars with their vast and incomprehensible distances that are being observed for the first time in all history by radio telescopes—then, if he is not blind, and if his eyes are opened by the Holy Spirit, he sees the glory of God. Both day and night reveal things about God, and so plainly, it is as if they had lips and tongues with which to talk. For David says further: "Day to day utters speech, and night to night shows knowledge" (Ps. 19:2). By simply observing these things, we learn about God as if nature had spoken of him. Paul asserts the same in Romans 1:20, where he says that certain invisible things of God, such as his power and divine nature, are clearly seen by observing the created world. For example, at about six years of age a boy will lose one of his teeth. Soon another one, a larger one, adapted to a growing jaw, will begin to appear, filling the space made by the lost tooth. When he realizes that it was God who caused the baby tooth to drop out at just the right time, not too early nor too late, and in exactly the right place, then he knows that God is a wise God. God revealed that to him through his tooth. Now that is an example of revelation, and by it man learns about God.

In this general revelation the Holy Spirit plays his part, as we have already seen in the chapter on "The Holy Spirit and Creation." There is a second revelation, too, called special revelation, that is, the Scriptures, in which the Holy Spirit plays a prominent role. It is interesting to note that even the first revelation, general revelation, cannot be read aright without knowing special revelation and without the illuminating power of the Spirit in man's mind. This is because of the spiritual blindness that has been caused by our own sin. Thus man cannot know a single thing of either general or special revelation without the Holy Spirit. The Spirit performs three works, all of which are essential for a true knowledge of the universe and the Creator. He reveals truth through general revelation, in which he is active. He also gives the Bible (special revelation), which is necessary in order to see aright the truths revealed in nature, and which is also necessary for a knowledge of great things not revealed in nature, such as the way of salvation, the nature of the church, and the second coming of Christ. Finally, he spiritually operates on man so that man can see the truths revealed in these two revelations.

Thus if man desires deep satisfaction in his soul, if he wants to have answered the deep questions that arise in every man at one time or another regardless of who he is or of the schooling he has had, he may have it. But he must know the Holy Spirit's work not only in general revelation, but also in special revelation; and he must experience the Spirit's activity in illuminating his mind, by which his spiritual blindness is removed. The Holy Spirit is the key to all true knowledge. Without him nothing can be fundamentally known. But with him man can have a knowledge of the universe and God that is eternally certain.

Let us, then, turn to these two other works of the Holy Spirit: the Bible and his illumination of the Christian's mind. Since the subject is so vast, in this chapter we shall deal only with the first work. In the next chapter we shall deal with the second one, the illumination by the Holy Spirit.

II. Special Revelation

There is a kind of special revelation which God gave to man apart from the Bible. From Paradise to Patmos, from Adam to John, God revealed himself to man in a special fashion. He did it in several ways.

He came in what are called *theophanies,* appearing in a visible form, for example, to Abraham, to Hagar, and to Jacob. He was revealed in the pillar of fire and cloud that protected and guided Israel in the wilderness. He also spoke directly to people of the Old and New Testaments: to Adam, Eve, Cain, Noah, Abraham, Jacob, Joseph, Moses, Samuel, and others. He spoke with a voice out of heaven. He appeared in dreams and in visions. He spoke by means of the Urim and Thummim. He gave direct communications to the prophets. And so, from Paradise to Patmos, God came in special, direct ways, revealing himself to men apart from the Bible.

Some of these revelations are of the greatest importance for us today. For example, the cultural commandments to Adam to be "fruitful, and multiply, and replenish the earth, and subdue it; and have dominion over" it (Gen. 1:28) have far-reaching implications for us. Or consider the great and first voice of the prophecy of the coming salvation, when God spoke to the serpent in the presence of Adam and Eve, saying: "I will put enmity between you and the woman, and between your seed and her seed. He will bruise your head, and you will bruise his heel" (Gen. 3:15). Or ponder the significance of the monumental covenant promise spoken to Abraham, when God said that he would be a God to him and to his seed after him. These and other revelations are matters of the utmost importance for the Christian. They give great and certain knowledge as to God's plans for eternity and as to his commands for us in such important fields as salvation and culture. This is what men of all ages have sought: certainty as to the future, and certainty as to present duties.

As far as we are concerned, however, there is one major limitation in all of these special revelations. God spoke. Nothing could be more certain. But once sin entered, would man be able to remember exactly what God said?

Granted, for example, that God did appear and speak in direct revelation to certain people in Bible times, what was the guarantee that that revelation would not be distorted by sinful man as it was passed down by word of mouth from Adam to Seth and through hundreds of generations down to us thousands of years later?

Or suppose that we do not go that far. Suppose, for example, you were in the place of Adam or Eve. Now Adam lived to be nine hundred and thirty years old. Assume further that eight hundred years after the fall you discussed with one or the other just what had happened and what was spoken by God in the garden. What do you think would happen after eight hundred years? There would undoubtedly be a conflict and misunderstanding as to exactly what God had said.

Or suppose you were with the Israelites when Moses gave to them the Ten Commandments, and after forty years of wandering in the wilderness you tried to recall precisely what Moses had said. The question might arise: Exactly what did Moses say? Did he say: Remember the sabbath day? or, Remember the sabbath day to keep it holy?

Or suppose that you had been in Peter's place on the mount of transfiguration with James, John, Moses, and Elijah; that you had seen Christ glorified and had heard the voice of the Father out of heaven. Could you have remembered ten years later all the events accurately, and could you guarantee that an account of them would be passed down infallibly to generations to come, by word of mouth?

Peter could not. He was with Christ. And yet he says in his Second Epistle that there is even "a more sure word of prophecy" (KJV)[1] (1:19). He was on the mount. He saw Christ. He heard God's voice out of heaven, and yet he says that in Scripture (prophecy) there is something that is more certain—more sure—than hearing the voice of God with his own ears and seeing Jesus with his own eyes. The implication is, of course, that time weakens the accuracy of the memory, so that a picture seen by the eye or a statement heard with the ear can be distorted over a period of time. But there is a prophecy that is more sure than his eyesight and his hearing, namely the Bible, which he goes on to describe in the next two verses. Because of the inspiration of the Holy Spirit, the accuracy of the statements of past events is guaranteed against faulty memory and against the errors that naturally develop in a secondhand or a thousandth-hand record.[2]

Peter thus saw clearly that, as wonderful as it might be for an individual to hear the voice of God, the certainty of it lasts only for that moment and for that individual. For us today, when God does not speak as in those days, we need the record in black and white, where we can go back again and again to ascertain exactly what was spoken. Now this is what the Bible gives us. It gives absolute certainty. It is as much the very words of God as if Christ should appear to you tonight in your room and should speak to you in a visible form, in a theophany.

Only, the Bible is better. For if Christ did speak to you, the voice would be gone again, once he had spoken. You could not go back and check the accuracy of your memory. Perhaps you would say later: Was that a dream or not? Did God actually speak or not? And what was it that he said, not vaguely, but accurately? Then you could never go back. You could never

[1] Prophecy must be taken in its official sense of speaking *for* God, not only of things in the future (predictions) but also of things that have already occurred or that are commandments of God.

[2] This argument is valid only if the Greek is translated as the Authorized Version has it, "a more sure word of prophecy." The comparison is then between the word on the Mount of Transfiguration and the word of prophecy. Many modern commentators, however, translate the passage as the American Standard Version has done, namely, "And we have the word of prophecy made more sure," i.e., confirmed by the word on the Mount.

repeat that blessed moment. But in the Bible God's voice remains recorded forever for you to return to repeatedly, to check precisely what he said. Thus if you want to hear the voice of God, his very words, and the actual message that is his alone, if you want this miracle, then go to the Bible and hear the Word of God. For the Word of God is a living miracle; it is God ever speaking to man, just as if he were speaking in a visible form to you in your own room.

III. The Spirit in Special Revelation

It is the Holy Spirit who is responsible for this remarkable miracle. It is he who gives us the voice of God so that, in the original languages, it is without one single error, recorded just exactly as God wanted it to be recorded. The Holy Spirit also gives to man the possibility of knowing eternal and temporal matters with absolute certainty.

That it is the Holy Spirit who inspired the Bible is the testimony of the Scriptures themselves. Peter states this very clearly when he says: "For prophecy never had its origin in the will of man, but men spoke from God as they were carried along by the Holy Spirit" (II Peter 1:21). Paul says that the things he speaks he speaks, "not in words taught us by human wisdom but in words taught by the Spirit, expressing spiritual truths in spiritual words" (I Cor. 2:13).

In many places in the New Testament the Holy Spirit is named as the author of an Old Testament portion. In Matthew 22:43 Jesus, quoting a psalm, said that David, in the Spirit, called the Messiah the Christ. On the occasion of the choosing of a disciple to replace Judas, Peter said: "Brothers, the Scripture had to be fulfilled which the Holy Spirit spoke long ago through the mouth of David concerning Judas . . ." (Acts 1:16). And the author of Hebrews, in quoting Psalm 95, introduces it by not even referring to the psalmist, but by saying: "So, as the Holy Spirit says" (Heb. 3:7), thus attributing to the Holy Spirit the authorship of the psalm. Constantly the Holy Spirit, and not the Father nor the Son, is referred to as the author of the Bible, although as we saw previously, we may never separate their work, since the Trinity is a unity.

The question now rises: How did the Holy Spirit inspire the Bible? How did he cause it to be the Word of God, God's own words, so that it is clothed with absolute authority? The Bible gives us hints concerning this process.

First of all, it was not done by the process of common grace. It was not done by the general operation of the Holy Spirit in the lives of the unregenerate, instilling new qualities in their minds so that their natural powers were sharpened to a high degree, enabling them to write works that were on the level of the so-called inspired works of Dante, Milton, or Shakespeare. The Bible was written by regenerate men, and the final product is one which is in a completely different category from all other writings. It has absolute authority because it is divinely inspired, and hence infallible.

Neither did the Holy Spirit produce the Bible by heightening the regenerative powers of man. For man is never made perfect in this life, but is sinful until death, even as is so obvious in David, Peter, and Paul. There have been many other holy men, such as Calvin and Luther, who were never inspired in this sense. Men are saints because they are mystically united to Christ Jesus, but some saints are writers of Scripture because they have been especially called by God to that particular task.

Neither does the evidence point to a mechanical method of dictation by the Holy Spirit. The Spirit did not appear in a vision to a few chosen individuals, nor whisper into their ears, so that these Biblical writers were nothing else than secretaries who did not use their minds, geniuses, or personalities in formulating the thoughts and words, but only mechanically pushed a pen as the Holy Spirit told them exactly what to write. This view ignores the obvious in Scripture—the differences in the various writings which cause even the untrained to say: "Now that sounds just like Paul," or "Isn't that like David?" If it is true that these different personal characteristics are seen in the various books of the Bible, then a person holding to the dictation theory must assume that the Holy Spirit dictated to his secretaries in such a way as to create the illusion that the words were formulated by the human authors, when in reality they proceeded from the Holy Spirit.

None of these theories is satisfactory. Rather, the Holy Spirit caused the Bible to be written in what is called an organic fashion. It was done more naturally, the way God so often works.

There is a passive side to the writing of the Bible, and an active side. In a certain sense the writers were completely passive. They did not cooperate with God so that they did half and God did the other half, nor so that God led them along and guided them, while they did most of the work. Rather, they were completely passive in the sense that Peter means when, in speaking about the sure prophetic word, he says: "For prophecy never had its origin in the will of man, but men spoke from God as they were carried along by the Holy Spirit" (II Peter 1:21). Man did not will it, the Holy Spirit did. Man had absolutely nothing to say in the decision to bring forth a Bible. God decided that. In other words, the human authors were the instruments by which God wrote. The Holy Spirit irresistibly caused them to write precisely what he wanted written, words of his own choosing. Furthermore, the word *carried* is a more faithful translation than the word *moved,* used in the King James and American Revised versions. It indicates the passivity of the Biblical authors. They were not partially active, being led or guided by the Holy Spirit. Rather, they were *carried,* which indicates that they contributed nothing to the process of being moved, but that they were the objects moved. A chair that is carried does not help in its being moved, does not will to be moved, does not contribute a single thing to the motion, but is completely helpless in the hands of the bearer. So also the prophets, says Peter, were carried by the Holy Spirit to write the things they wrote. They were passive.

This is also indicated by Paul's statement in II Timothy 3:16, where he says that "All scripture is God-breathed." This verse is often translated as "Every scripture is given by inspiration of God," but, as Warfield points out, it is more accurately translated, "All scripture is God-breathed." It is the breath of God; it is a completely divine product. This being so, the Bible is not something that men decided to produce on their own accord, but they received it from the Holy Spirit. It is a divine product, and they were passive in its making.

Although there is a passive side to the writing of the Bible, there is also an active side. It is this that we must now stress if we are to do justice to the process of inscripturation, and if we are to see the full manner in which the Holy Spirit breathed out the Scriptures.

The writing of the Bible might be compared to the salvation of a believer, in a certain sense. In one sense it may be said that salvation is wholly of God. It is something that man receives. Man is passive, and God is active in working it out in man. Yet,

in another sense, man is very active. Although his whole salvation, including faith, is a gift which is wholly of God; and although "it is God who works in you to will and to act according
to his good purposes" (Phil. 2:13), so that man is entirely, re-
ceptively passive; yet the immediately preceding clause presents
the active side of salvation in the command to "work out your
salvation with fear and trembling." God does not regenerate men
by treating them as mere machines that have no mind or will. He
does not do away with their previous experiences and characteristics when he regenerates them, so that they lose all those particular qualities that make Mr A. so different from Mr. B. All
Christians are not dull, stereotyped characters with no distinc-
tiveness about them. They are not like little toy soldiers made by
a machine, with no difference in them at all—all painted the
same color, all the same height, all with a gun on the shoulder,
all with the same foot forward. No, God retains all of man's
distinctive talents, individuality, and characteristics, and these
go to make up the life of the Christian. Man receives salvation;
he is passive. But he is also very active, believing in Christ and
living the Christian life in his own way according to his distinguishing characteristics.

In a similar fashion was the composing of the Bible accomplished. The authors were entirely passive. The Bible is a divine
product. It did not come by the will of man, but men of God
spoke as they were carried by the Holy Spirit. Yet God did not
destroy the authors' individuality and talents, making the whole
Bible stereotyped, with only one style from Genesis to Revelation—the style of the Holy Spirit—with all the human differences
of the writers overridden and ignored. Rather, God allowed
the experiences of the authors to govern their writing, their
differing emotions to color their thinking, their individual tastes
to be expressed in the Bible. He permitted David's love for
nature to shine forth in his psalms, Paul's acquaintance with
pagan literature to be evident in his Epistles, Luke's medical
knowledge to characterize his writings, Mark's abruptness to be
in his book, whereas Paul wrote in a logical manner and John in
a more mystical fashion.

At the same time that the authors were 100 percent passive,
they were also 100 percent active. They were not forced to write
messages against their wills, any more than an unbeliever is
forced to believe against his will. God creates the circumstances

in just such a way that when he regenerates an unbeliever's heart, he naturally causes him to want to leave his pleasurable sins and accept Christ as his Savior. In a similar fashion, God has a message—an exact one, with precise wording—that he wants written without a single error even to the dotting of the "i's" or the crossing of the "t's" (Christ says "jots and tittles"). So he prepares humans to do this for him willingly and actively.

Centuries before Moses was born, God molded great-grand-mothers and great-grandfathers who would pass down to Moses just the right hereditary characteristics to make him write with a certain slant, naturally, and not in a forced way. The exact mother and father were chosen to give that certain training which would enable him to write with the precise emotions that the Holy Spirit wanted. A persecution was brought on so that Moses, hidden and found in a basket, might be brought up in the Egyptian culture, for the Holy Spirit wanted him to learn to read and write and to have a legal training so that he could write the Pentateuch. Then God controlled the circumstances around the killing of an Egyptian which forced Moses into the wilderness to be alone for years in order to learn humility and devotion so that he could write the Pentateuch in that spirit, too.

Then, when God had prepared all the circumstances in just the right way—when Moses had just the right hereditary influences and the proper characteristics, when his life had been molded by just the experiences that the Spirit wanted—under the Spirit's influence, Moses began to write exactly what the Holy Spirit wanted. And it was not done in a forced way of mechanical dictation, as if the Holy Spirit whispered into his ear what to write. But, influenced in the minutest detail by the many factors and experiences of his life, which had been purposely arranged by God, Moses wrote naturally and expressed himself just as he would in normal life. Thus, using his own mind, resources, and individual characteristics, he wrote the very words that the Holy Spirit desired. Of course, as he wrote, Moses also received from the Holy Spirit direct revelations about things that he did not know, such as the creation of the world or prophecies; and the Spirit superintended his writing so that errors which normally creep into a person's writings were kept from his.

The finished product was truly Moses' work. *He* did it. Moses was not just a secretary or a pen by which the Holy Spirit wrote, but Moses contributed his own thinking and experiences. He was 100 percent active. At the same time, however, since God had controlled all the factors that influenced Moses to write precisely as he did, what Moses wrote was also a divine product; it was the breath of God, God-breathed. It was the book of the Holy Spirit in all of its parts. In this sense Moses was also 100 percent passive. The Pentateuch was the word of Moses at the same time that it was the Word of God.

Conclusion

The result of this activity and control of the Holy Spirit is a book that is to other books what the man Jesus is to other men. As the people noticed that Jesus was one who spoke, not as other men, not as the scribes, but as one with authority; so we notice, too, that the Bible speaks, not as other books, but with authority. As Jesus was one who not only had a human nature but also a divine one, so the Bible has not only a human nature, in that it was written by men, but also a divine nature, in that it was written by God. Just as Jesus is the Word of God, so also is the Bible. And just as Jesus is the Lord of lords, so also is the Bible the Book of books.

The Bible, then, is the very word of God, and not simply a record of that word. It is God speaking to men every day. It is a living miracle of the breath of God. And it is for this reason, as we mentioned at the start of this chapter, that man can have the absolute certainty that the philosophers of all ages have sought. By going to the Bible he can have the true and certain knowledge, which gives deep satisfaction to that natural craving of man. Therefore, let us again praise the Holy Spirit for his third stupendous work: not only for his finishing work in creation, nor simply for his pervasive activity in the realm of common grace, which makes this world livable, but also for making it possible for us to hear right now, and as long as we live, the voice of God, which is permanently and infallibly recorded in the Bible.

The Holy Spirit and Illumination 5

In the last chapter we saw that revelation is the source of all knowledge. God has given man two kinds of revelation: general and special. General revelation is that which is found in every part of the created world. Special revelation is the Bible. These two revelations are the source of all knowledge. Although general revelation is the source of knowledge, it cannot be read aright without the Bible. We developed the fact that the Bible, through the comprehensive work of the Holy Spirit, is the continual voice of God and is without error. If any man would have true knowledge, he must go to these two revelations, and there he can arrive at certainty in his mind.

We intimated, however, that it is not sufficient for our knowledge to have an external, objective revelation where truth is infallibly recorded. This was adequate at one time before sin entered the world, in the day of the innocency of Adam and Eve. But once sin entered the world, both general and special revelation became insufficient to give true knowledge. Not that these two revelations were insufficient in themselves, nor that they were in any way defective. For they were not. As far as general revelation is concerned, the created world revealed clearly the invisible

53

things of God (Rom. 1:20). As far as special revelation is concerned, the Holy Spirit gave to us a Bible that in the original languages is infallible in the very words and even the jots and tittles. The revelations are perfect, clear, and plain. The defect is not in them. They are perfectly sufficient to supply man with absolute knowledge.

The fault lies, however, with man, and in this chapter we will see how the giving of the eyes, or the illumination of the mind so that man can read the Bible aright, is also the work of the Holy Spirit.

First of all, we should notice that man is in need of spiritual illumination. Second, we should notice that the Holy Spirit is the only one who can fill that need.

I. Man's Blindness

The New Testament intimates that natural man is blind, blind as a mole, so that he cannot see the great and clear truths even when they are presented to him by an apostle. Luke relates that Lydia, along with other women at the riverside, heard Paul preach, and that the Lord opened her heart to respond to the things Paul spoke (Acts 16:14). The clear implication is that, as she first listened, she could understand nothing. She was dull of heart spiritually. Her understanding was darkened, to use Paul's description of the Gentile Ephesians (Eph. 4:18). She could understand the Greek that was spoken, but not the real meaning of the words. But when the Lord opened her heart, she was then enabled to respond to the things spoken. Without the Lord she had no spiritual understanding. She was blind.

Paul describes the blindness of the soul as a veil on the heart (II Cor. 3:12-18). In speaking about the unconverted Jews, he says that their minds are blinded. When the writings of Moses are read to them they cannot understand. This lack of understanding is not because Moses' writings are difficult, but rather because there is a veil or covering on their hearts. The veil is there because they are not regenerated, for, says Paul, "Whenever anyone turns to the Lord, the veil is taken away" (v. 16) and they understand.

Perhaps the passage of Scripture that is the clearest in showing the inability of the natural man to understand spiritual things is I Corinthians 1 and 2. There Paul says that those who are the reprobate consider the gospel to be nonsense when they come in contact with it, "for the message of the cross is foolishness to those who are perishing" (1:18). The natural man cannot understand it. If he could, then there would be many wise ones, many noble and mighty ones who would be Christians. But such is not the case. "Brothers, think of what you were when you were called. Not many of you were wise by human standards; not many were influential; not many were of noble birth" (1:26). The reason the brilliant minds do not accept Christianity is that all minds are blind, regardless of their I.Q., unless they are regenerated. For, Paul asserts in unequivocal terms, "the man without the Spirit does not accept the things that come from the Spirit of God" (2:14). He does not say "the unintelligent man" or "the uneducated" or "the uncultured," but simply "the man without the Spirit." Regardless of his natural intelligence, the natural man simply "does not accept the things that come from the Spirit of God." He considers them to be "foolishness." He rejects the creation account as contrary to obvious scientific facts. He considers the history of Adam and Eve and the serpent as a fairy tale. That the New Testament claims that Jesus is God he attributes to simple authors in the later church who did not know better. The substitutionary atonement is ridiculous to him. Predestination and human responsibility are obviously incompatible. That an omnipotent and yet holy God foreordains sin he considers preposterous. So, professing himself to be wise, he becomes a fool (Rom. 1:22), considering the things of the Spirit of God as foolishness (I Cor. 2:14). Paul then emphatically reaffirms this same teaching by stating, "and he cannot understand them." It is impossible for him to understand them. The reason is, Paul goes on to say, that the things of God are spiritually discerned, that is, only a person who has the Spirit of God can understand them. And since natural man does not have the Holy Spirit, he cannot understand them.

Although the Bible tells us that man without the Spirit is totally blind, it must not be presumed that the regenerate has 20-20 vision. The psalmist says, "Open my eyes that I may see wonderful things out of your law" (119:18). There are wonderful things in the Old Testament. They are plain to anyone who can see. They are there before the psalmist. He does not ask for something in addition to the law. But he cannot see what is in front of him. So he prays that God will open his spiritual eyes so that he can see these "wonderful things." In a word, David was in part spiritually blind even though he was regenerated.

The New Testament, also, implies the partial blindness of the Christian. Luke, in relating the events before the ascension, says that as Jesus was telling his disciples about the prophecies in the Old Testament, "he opened their minds so they could understand the Scriptures" (Luke 24:45). In other words, before Jesus opened their minds they could not understand the Scriptures, even though they might have read them a hundred times. Their minds were closed.

In Ephesians 1:17-19 Paul prays: "I keep asking that the God of our Lord Jesus Christ, the glorious Father, may give you the Spirit of wisdom and revelation, so that you may know him better. I pray also that the eyes of your heart may be enlightened in order that you may know the hope to which he has called you, the riches of his glorious inheritance in the saints, and his incomparably great power for us who believe." These great blessings were before these regenerated Ephesians and were even being experienced by them, yet they did not know them fully; they could not see them. It was not because the Ephesians were not intelligent or not educated, for we have reason to believe that they were men of learning. Neither was it because Paul had not told them about these truths, for in Acts 20 we read that Paul had taught them the whole counsel of God night and day with tears for three years. But it was because they were still partially blind. Even though they were Christians, and therefore born again and translated out of the kingdom of darkness into the kingdom of light, yet they retained a certain amount of blindness. So Paul prayed that God might give them the Spirit of wisdom and revelation, that their eyes might be enlightened in order to see the riches of the gospel of Christ Jesus.

Thus the unmistakable teaching of Scripture is that wisdom is found in God's twofold revelation: the created world and the Bible. These are clear. But sin has darkened man's mind. The regenerate man, in whom the Holy Spirit has begun his sanctifying work, can see at least a beginning of these truths, but the man without the Spirit can see nothing. He should be able to see these truths in God's revelation, for they are absolutely plain. But he cannot. Take a person out on a cloudless twenty-first of June, when the sun is at its meridian, tell him to look around, and ask him what he sees. If he says he does not see a thing, then you can be sure that he is blind, totally blind. In the same fashion, present to a man the crystal-clear Word of God, which plainly testifies to the deity of Jesus Christ, the sin of man, and to Christ as the only way of salvation; and then ask him whether he acknowledges these truths. If he says: "I can't see them as truths; they are fairy tales, figments of men's imagination, plain ordinary nonsense that only the ignorant believe in," then you know that that man is blind, too, stone blind. He cannot see a thing. He should be able to see, because Scripture cannot be plainer. It is just as brilliant as the sun. If he does not see the truths, then it is only because of his own spiritual blindness. As Scripture says: The man without the Spirit does not accept the things that come from the Spirit of God. A veil has covered his heart. His eyes are closed.

II. The Spirit's Illumination

To have true knowledge, then, it is not enough to have God's clear revelation; man must also be able to see. And it is exactly at this point that the Holy Spirit enters in, too. He gives man not only an infallible book, but also eyes so that he can read that book.

Some of the passages already mentioned show clearly that the opening of one's spiritual eyes is an act of God and not of man. The psalmist, feeling his inability to open his eyes by himself, prays to God to do it when he petitions: "Open my eyes that I may see wonderful things out of your law" (119:18). He has tried to do it himself. He cannot. So he asks God, the only one who can, to open his eyes. Likewise, Luke said that it was the Lord who opened the eyes of his disciples so that they could understand; and we read that it was the Lord who opened Lydia's heart so that she could comprehend.

More specifically, however, it is the third Person of the Trinity, and not the Father nor the Son, who illuminates man's mind. Just as he is the One who gives natural understanding and wisdom in the first place (see chapter 2), so he is also the One who restores this wisdom after man has fallen.

This is abundantly clear from especially five passages of Scripture. In I Corinthians 2 Paul declares that he did not come to Corinth "with eloquence or superior wisdom" (v. 1), and, he continues, "my message and my preaching were not with wise and persuasive words, but with a demonstration of the Spirit's power, so that your faith might not rest on men's wisdom, but on God's power" (2:4, 5). In other words, Paul, or any man for that matter, does not impart faith and the knowledge that is necessary for faith by great oratory, eloquence, and logic. Rather, that faith comes by the demonstration and power of the Holy Spirit. He is the One who comes into hearts in an indescribable, mysterious way, who irresistibly convinces a person of the truth of the gospel, and who thereby causes him to believe. Hence the Corinthians' faith does not stand in such an evanescent thing as the wisdom of men, but rather in the power of the Holy Spirit.

Later on in this very chapter Paul reaffirms the same point by contrasting the natural and the spiritual man (2:14, 15). The natural man, as we have seen, is blind, and therefore cannot receive the things of the Spirit of God. But "the spiritual man makes judgments about all things" (2:15). When speaking of a "spiritual" person, Paul means that person who is indwelt by the Holy Spirit. Only such a person, says Paul, can discern all things. Therefore, the Holy Spirit is necessary for the enlightenment of one's mind.

In Ephesians 1:18 Paul is also unequivocal as to the fact that it is the Holy Spirit who enlightens the mind. For he prays, not that the intellect of the believers might be sharpened—nor for new knowledge—but he prays specifically for the Spirit of wisdom and revelation that "the eyes of their heart" may be enlightened so that they may know the things of the Spirit of God.

To the Thessalonians he writes that the gospel did not come to them in word only, either by letter or by word of mouth, but it was accompanied by the power of the Spirit, so that it was received with great joy (I Thess. 1:5, 6).

Finally, John writes that his readers "have an anointing," that is, the Holy Spirit is in them. The result is, he writes, that "all of you know the truth" (I John 2:20) and that "you do not need anyone to teach you," but "his anointing teaches you about all things" (v. 27).

The sum of the matter is, then, that when the Holy Spirit comes into people's lives he enlightens them, gives them understanding, teaches them, opens their eyes, removes the veil from their hearts, and softens their hearts so that they can know the things of the Spirit of God. Without him, man is blind to see the

truths of revelation; but when there is a demonstration of the
Spirit and of power, man knows all things.

It should be carefully observed that the Holy Spirit does not
enlighten man by giving to him a secret revelation—new knowledge. There have been no more revelations since the completion
of the Bible. Special revelation was closed with the New Testament. Furthermore, to give a new revelation would be as useless
as trying to make a blind man see by placing two suns in the sky
instead of one. No, the Holy Spirit enlightens man, not by giving
him added content of knowledge, but by mysteriously operating
on his heart so he can see the revelation already given. The
psalmist did not need another law, but an opening of his eyes
to see the law already there before him. The unconverted Jews
did not need additional revelations to those of Moses, but a
removal of the veil from their hearts. The Ephesians did not
need another gospel, but the dispelling of the darkness that
prevented them from seeing the gospel that Paul had already
preached to them.

When Paul writes to the Thessalonians that "our gospel came
to you not simply with words, but also with power, with the
Holy Spirit and with deep conviction," he does not say that he
gave them a new message, but that the old one came in a new
way. In a similar fashion, the reason that the Corinthian Christians could understand the gospel, while other wise ones could
not, was not that a new revelation had been given, but that the
old one had come "with a demonstration of the Spirit's power."

And in Jesus' parable of the rich man and Lazarus, what the
rich man's brothers needed for their conversion was not more
knowledge or a proof by a man rising from the dead. No, they
had Moses and the Prophets. What they needed was a spiritual
awakening and illumination so they could believe what was
already in the Bible.

This illumination might be compared to the opening of
Balaam's eyes when the angel of the Lord stood in his path.
The angel was there, and the donkey could see him, but Balaam
could not. In order to make Balaam see, God did not have to
place another angel before him, but he simply had to open his
eyes that he might see the one who was already there.

Or this enlightenment might be likened to the effect of a
telescope. Without it, man does not see those stars out in infinity.
But they are there nevertheless. What he needs is a new eye,

a telescope, so that he can see what is right in front of him. The telescope does not place a new object before a person, but it makes visible what is already there.

And so it is with the illumination by the Holy Spirit. The Spirit opens man's spiritual eyes to see the revelation which is already before him. A thousand new revelations will not help the man to see if he cannot even see one. Illumination, then, consists, not of the giving of a new knowledge content, but of the opening of man's eyes to see what is plainly before him.

Conclusion

These facts explain what would otherwise be enigmas. It is sometimes thought that if Christianity is so good, if it offers the greatest benefits in this world and the world to come, if it is so logical, if it is the fountain of all true knowledge, then why do not more people believe? Why are the churches not made up mostly of college graduates and professional men? Why do not the educated flock to church?

The answer is, of course, that becoming a Christian does not depend upon man's wisdom but upon the illuminating work of the Holy Spirit so that the spiritually blind may see.

It is for the same reason that at times some of the most unlikely people accept Christ. We sometimes look at a person from a human point of view and judge to ourselves: "That person is hopeless. He is too tough to become a Christian. He does not care. He is too calloused in sin. He swears terribly. And his life is scandalous." And yet, to our amazement, that person becomes receptive to the gospel. He, a hardened sinner who never shed a tear in his life, comes to Christ with tears in his eyes. He can no more resist the offer of salvation than a daisy can resist being crushed by an elephant's foot. This is because Christianity does not depend on man, but on the Holy Spirit. You see, it makes no difference if a person is a genius or a hardened criminal. His wisdom will not save and his hardness will not damn. But if the Holy Spirit works within his heart, his heart becomes softened, melted—or, as Ezekiel put it, the heart of stone becomes a heart of flesh—all resistance has melted and the person accepts Christ. Salvation depends on God and not on man.

Therefore, if we are to win souls to Christ, we must pray that the Holy Spirit will enlighten the one with whom we are working. Otherwise our efforts will be of no avail. We may take an unconverted friend to hear the most eloquent and popular preacher possible, we may reason with him with the greatest logic (and Christianity has dazzling logic), we may approach him in the most subtle, unoffensive, and tactful fashion, we may talk to him until we have no breath left, but it will be of absolutely no avail if the Holy Spirit is not opening his eyes and removing the veil from his heart so that he can see the truth and believe. Thus in the winning of souls a prime prerequisite is praying for the Holy Spirit to open the heart of the unconverted. And when that happens, even our bungling stupidity cannot prevent him from understanding. Maybe much of our discouragement in the winning of souls is due to the fact that in presenting tracts and in witnessing we have not prayed for the enlightening work of the Holy Spirit in the life of the one with whom we are dealing.

As far as our own understanding is concerned, we must pray for the Holy Spirit, too. Remember that the Ephesians to whom Paul wrote were already Christians. They were the ones to whom Paul wrote that glorious first chapter, showing them that the foundation of their faith was in the eternal, predestinating love of God. Yet he prays in that same chapter that God may grant them the Spirit of wisdom and revelation so that, the eyes of their understanding being enlightened, they might know the glories of the gospel of Christ. And so with us too, we still have considerable dimness in our eyes (some more than others); we still are not free from blindness; we still cannot see as well as we should. So we should pray constantly as Christians that the Spirit of wisdom and revelation will come and illuminate our minds so that we may see more of the great truths of revelation.

Thus, in conclusion to both the last chapter and this one: Christianity has the secret of all true knowledge. This secret depends on the twofold operation of the Holy Spirit. It depends on his work in the Bible, the eternal voice of God, which is the source of all knowledge, even of the correct interpretation of natural revelation; and it depends on the illumination of one's mind by the Holy Spirit. If a person relies on these workings of the Spirit, he may achieve what philosophers have sought for in all ages: true knowledge. And he will be satisfied.

The Holy Spirit and Jesus Christ

6

To one not thoroughly acquainted with the work of the Holy Spirit, it is nothing short of amazing to discover what a great role he plays in this universe. To one accustomed to thinking of the Holy Spirit only in terms of regeneration and sanctification, it is somewhat startling to realize that he is also the perfecter of creation, the mediator of common grace, the author of special revelation, and the effectual founder of the church of Christ. In this chapter we come to still another great work of the Holy Spirit: his activity in the life of our God and Savior, Jesus Christ.

To understand the work of the Holy Spirit in Christ Jesus, it is necessary to recall the Biblical conception of Christ. He is the second Person of the Godhead and is eternally begotten of the Father. He is fully God: eternal, incomprehensible, all-powerful, all-knowing, and everywhere present. In the fullness of time he voluntarily came to earth and assumed a human nature, so that he could be called at the same time God and man. Remaining God, he became, in addition, man. He was different from anyone else who has ever lived on earth in that he was not only a complete man but also fully God.

Because of this great truth, Christians have sometimes doubted the necessity of the work of the Holy Spirit in Christ. If Christ is God himself, some reason, he does not need the Holy Spirit. He can do all things necessary by virtue of the fact that he is God. Therefore, the Holy Spirit is relegated to a negligible role in the life of Christ.

But this is a mistake caused either by an overemphasizing of the Godhead of Christ or a minimizing of his manhood. As far as the divine nature of Jesus is concerned—his deity—the Holy Spirit has little influence. For the second Person of the Trinity is coequal with the third. But as far as the human nature of Christ is concerned—his manhood—he does need the constant presence of the Holy Spirit.

Jesus remained complete man at the same time that he was complete God. The fact that his human nature was indivisible and inseparable from his divine nature did not mean that his human nature changed and became fused with the divine nature. (For a beautiful, short formulation of this, read the carefully worded Symbol of Chalcedon, written in 451.) The union of the two natures did not mean that his divine nature gave divine qualities, such as omnipotence or omniscience, to his human nature, with the result that Jesus ceased to be truly man and was only God. There was no transference of the divine characteristics of the Godhead to the human nature or manhood of Christ, so that Jesus ended up with two divine natures, instead of one divine and one human nature. His divine nature did not deify his human nature. Rather, the Scriptures tell us that Jesus, remaining God, was also so completely man that he grew from a baby to a boy to a man, that he was tempted in all points as we are (Heb. 4:15), that he did not know the day or the hour of his second coming (Mark 13:32), and that he was forsaken by God on the cross (Matt. 27:46). The distinction of his two natures remained. He was at the same time completely God and completely man, eternal and yet finite.

Since Jesus was also complete man, there was room for the work of the Holy Spirit in his whole life. The Bible amply indicates that this is so. As the Christian reads his Bible, he will notice that the Holy Spirit was operative in the life of Christ Jesus from his incarnation to his ultimate glory. We will now proceed to see how this can be.

I. His Incarnation

The Holy Spirit was needed at the very start of Jesus' human life, at his incarnation. By the word *incarnation* we mean that act by which the second Person of the Trinity, remaining God, "became flesh and lived for a while among us" (John 1:14). This was an act effected by the Holy Spirit, as is seen by both Matthew's statement that Mary "was found to be with child through the Holy Spirit" (1:18), and the angel's announcement to Mary that the "Holy Spirit will come upon you, and the power of the Most High will overshadow you" (Luke 1:35). The Holy Spirit is the cause of the conception of Jesus. He is the one, and not the Father nor the Son, let alone Joseph, who planted the seed of life in a mysterious way in Mary's womb.

This does not mean that the other Persons of the Trinity had no part in the incarnation. For, as we saw in the matter of creation, all three Persons are active in all things in this world. Yet it is possible on the basis of Scripture to say that two Persons of the Trinity work through the other one. This is true with the conception of Jesus. It was an act of the Triune God. The Father was a coauthor of the incarnation, as is evidenced by Christ's words to the Father when he said: "Sacrifice and offering you did not desire, but a body you prepared for me" (Heb. 10:5). In other words, the Father prepared Christ's human nature (here called the body). The Son was also a coauthor of his own incarnation (becoming flesh). He was not passively born, as we are, but actively so. He willingly and voluntarily chose to be conceived in Mary's womb. Paul reveals this when he says that Christ, "being in very nature God, did not consider equality with God something to be grasped, but made himself nothing, taking the very nature of a servant, being made in human likeness" (Phil. 2:6, 7). In short, Christ and the Father, as well as the Spirit, were active in Christ's coming to earth.

Although the incarnation was an act of all three Persons of the Godhead, yet it was especially the work of the Holy Spirit. He, and not the Father nor the Son, was the efficient cause by which Mary was found with child. He was "the power of the Most High," as Luke puts it, that effected the conception of Jesus. As the Apostles' Creed confesses, Jesus was conceived not by the Father nor by himself, but by the Holy Spirit. Therefore, in this special sense, the Holy Spirit was the originator and efficient cause of the incarnation.

Note that although Jesus was conceived by the Holy Spirit, so that he could be called a "child of the Holy Spirit" (Matt. 1:18, KJV), this does not mean that the Spirit was the father of Jesus. Fatherhood depends upon more than causing something to be. Otherwise, a model airplane could be called the son of a boy, or a dress could be called the daughter of a seamstress. The relation of the Holy Spirit to the human nature of Christ is that of Creator and creature. It is the first Person of the Trinity, not the third, who is Christ's Father.

This conceiving act of the Holy Spirit was essential in order to secure Christ's sinlessness, which, in turn, was necessary in order for him to become our Savior. It preserved Christ from that original sin which is the lot of every person born into this world. Through man's conception and birth, he is unholy, full of blame, impure, and one with other sinners. Through Christ's conception he was "holy, blameless, pure, and set apart from sinners" (Heb. 7:26). Man is conceived and born in sin (Ps. 51:5), but Christ was conceived and born in holiness.

To develop this further, every man inherits the two elements of original sin: first, a guilt which he inherits from Adam, who acted as his representative in the Garden of Eden; and, second, a corrupt nature that is inclined to all evil. This original sin is his before he himself is capable of actually sinning. It comes by virtue of his birth. And then, if God does not intervene, that corrupt nature with which he is born, and which at first seems so innocent, unfolds in all its hideousness.

Because of his conception by the Holy Spirit, Christ was preserved from this twofold aspect of original sin. He, and not Mary, was immaculately[1] conceived. He was true man and "has been tempted in every way, just as we are—yet was without sin" (Heb. 4:15). He "had no sin" (II Cor. 5:21), "committed no sin" (I Peter 2:22), was as "a lamb without blemish or defect" (I Peter 1:19), and was "holy, blameless, pure, and set apart from sinners" (Heb. 7:26).

This means that in at least the two ways in which man be-

---

[1] The Roman Catholic Church teaches as an infallible truth that Mary was immaculately conceived, that is, she "was preserved free from all stain of original sin."

comes a sinner by birth, Christ was sinless by his birth. He did not inherit the guilt of Adam's representative sin, as do all other men (Rom. 5:12 ff.), nor did he receive a human nature that was morally corrupt; rather, his human nature was spotless and morally beautiful. And this spotless purity of Christ was due to the operation of the Holy Spirit whereby Jesus was immaculately and miraculously conceived without Joseph's taking part.

Thus the Holy Spirit was necessary in Christ's life from its very inception. He was necessary for two reasons: first, in order that Christ might be born; and, second, in order that his human nature might be preserved from the guilt and corruption of Adam's sin so that he could be our Savior.

II. His Indwelling by the Holy Spirit

Not only did the Holy Spirit keep Jesus from taint of sin in any form whatsoever, but also, he was the author of holiness in Jesus' human nature. This is implied, of course, when it is stated that Jesus was free from sin. For if one is without sin, he must be completely holy. There can be no vacuum in the soul. The absence of evil means the presence of holiness.

That the Holy Spirit is the author of holiness in Jesus' human nature is also implied by the fact, as we have already seen, that the Holy Spirit is the author of all life, both natural and spiritual. He is the giver of intellectual, aesthetic, and moral attainments. This is true of Christ's human nature as well as of men in general.

Furthermore, in speaking of Jesus, John specifically records that "to him God gives the Spirit without limit" (3:34). To us God gives the Spirit in part and never in fullness, but to Christ he gave without limit, in completion and fullness. This refers, naturally, only to Christ as man, and not as God. And this means, furthermore, that the Holy Spirit dwelt in Jesus Christ as man. The Holy Spirit came and lived in Christ much the same as he dwells in the Christian. In fact, Jesus may have spoken of this indwelling when he referred to his body as a temple that he would raise three days after its destruction by the Jews.

III. His Growth

Although it is true that the Spirit dwelt without limit in Jesus as a man, it is also true that there was growth in Christ's spiritual life. This is one of the most fascinating accounts in Scripture and one that is often denied, especially by those who, out of re-action to Modernism, desire to safeguard the deity of Christ against all attacks.

Luke reveals this growth very pointedly when he says: "And the child grew and became strong; he was filled with wisdom, and the grace of God was upon him" (2:40). It is likely that Luke meant that "the child grew" physically, and "became strong" intellectually and morally, since it would be repetitious to have both the growing and the becoming strong refer to the same thing, his physical life. Furthermore, in Luke 1:80 these same words ("and the child grew and became strong") are used of John the Baptist, with the addition of the words "in the spirit" after the phrase "he became strong." This development is also confirmed by verse 52, where Luke says that "Jesus grew in wisdom and stature, and in favor with God and men."

In other words, Luke tells us that there was a growth in Jesus' intellectual and spiritual life. He was not born an adult as Adam was, so he had to pretend to be a baby, but he was born as a real infant. He had to grow as a normal child from the stage of infancy to the creeping age, to a walking and talking child, to a growing and learning boy, until he reached full manhood. In one chapter, the second, Luke calls Christ first a baby (verses 12 and 16), then a child (verse 40), then a boy (verse 43), and finally Jesus (verse 52). This indicates that Jesus was truly man, and his human nature was not endowed, through its union with the divine nature, with divine attributes such as all-powerfulness, all-knowingness, and infinity. Rather, he was born a baby, as the Bible says. He grew in wisdom, as verses 40 and 52 expressly state. He increased in spirituality. And because of all this he actually "grew . . . in favor with God." This great mystery can be partially understood if we remember that all of this growth applied only to Jesus' human nature. His Godhead, of course, could not grow one whit in any sense, since that always has been complete.

All of this growth was due to the Holy Spirit. It was not an automatic growth. Nor was it due to the fact that the man Jesus was inseparably connected with the divine person, so that as a man he had omniscience. For that would destroy the true humanity of Jesus. And the Bible tells us that even when he was an adult in his full ministry, he did not know the exact date of his own second coming. Rather, this spiritual and intellectual growth was due to the operation of the Holy Spirit in the life of Christ. Isaiah predicted this when he wrote: "And there will come forth a shoot [i.e., Jesus] out of the stock of Jesse, and a branch out of his roots will bear fruit. And the Spirit of the LORD will rest on him, the Spirit of wisdom and understanding, the Spirit of counsel and might, the Spirit of knowledge and of the fear of the LORD" (11:1, 2). In short, it was the Holy Spirit who came on Jesus, as far as his human nature was concerned, and caused him as a little baby and a boy to become strong, and grow in wisdom, in stature, and in favor with God and men. As a growing lad Jesus needed the Holy Spirit.

If someone should be puzzled how Jesus could be filled with the Spirit without measure (John 3:34) and yet grow spiritually, the answer is not far to find. It lies in the distinction between the perfection of innocency and the perfection of holiness, and in the fact that Jesus grew from a baby to full manhood. A baby, such as Jesus, may have the fullness of the Spirit, and yet not exercise that holiness. He may have a perfection of innocency, while the adult may have the perfection of holiness. The baby Jesus had all the inclinations and will to holiness, but simply because he was an infant he could not exercise the intellect and will of his human nature as could an adult. As a baby he could not even talk, for example—let alone reason with the theologians, as he did when he was twelve years old. He could not be confronted with choices of right and wrong for the reason that his human mind was not developed enough even to understand the ethical problems involved. All the time, however, even as a baby, he was indwelt by the Spirit. Jesus' nature and disposition were completely holy, even if they could not express themselves. This holy nature was latent, and the exercise of it would come only as his mind grew and developed. He had to learn, for example, obedience (Heb. 5:8)—not that he was ever disobedient and thereby sinful. He was not. But he had to develop that innate holy disposition that the Holy Spirit had planted within him, but which, while he was a baby, could not come to fruition.

So we see that not only was the Holy Spirit necessary for Jesus' conception and birth, but he was also necessary for the whole period of growth as a child and as a maturing young man.

IV. His Baptism

Another evidence of the work of the Holy Spirit in the life of Christ is seen at his baptism, when he was consecrated and empowered by the Holy Spirit to begin his public ministry as the Mediator. Even after Jesus had been filled with the Spirit of wisdom and understanding, and had advanced in the favor of God in his own personal life, he still needed the Holy Spirit in a new way for his public life. Apart from his holy life, he needed the Spirit in order that he might be equipped with the necessary qualifications to discharge his office as Messiah—as prophet, priest, and king.

This endowment by the Holy Spirit came at his baptism. We read that as Jesus was baptized "the heaven was opened, and the Holy Spirit descended on him in bodily form like a dove" (Luke 3:21, 22). Before this event, we read nothing of Jesus' ministry in all the gospels; rather, we read only about his birth and boyhood. Afterwards we hear about his ministry of preaching and performing miracles. And immediately after Luke's record of baptism, he tells us expressly that Jesus began to teach, being about thirty years old (3:23). Thus we conclude that the giving of the Holy Spirit to Christ at baptism was for the purpose of officially equipping him for his public ministry.

Jesus was conscious of this anointing by the Holy Spirit for his official ministry. For, right after his baptism by the Spirit, he delivered his first sermon at Nazareth, using as his text Isaiah 61:1, where the prophet wrote: "The Spirit of the Lord is on me; therefore he has anointed me to preach good news to the poor. He has sent me to proclaim freedom for the prisoners and recovery of sight for the blind, to release the oppressed, to proclaim the year of the Lord's favor" (Luke 4:18, 19). After he sat down he said, "Today this scripture is fulfilled in your hearing." In other words, the Holy Spirit had come upon him at that time to empower him to preach the gospel in his public ministry.

That the Holy Spirit also gave him special powers to perform miracles for his ministry is seen in one of his struggles with the Pharisees when he said: "If I drive out demons by the Spirit of God, then the kingdom of God has come upon you" (Matt. 12:28). He then lets the Jews know that by calling him Beelzebub, the prince of the devils, they are blaspheming chiefly against the Holy Spirit, since it was the Holy Spirit who was really the author of those miracles, even if they were done through Jesus.

Here again, we see clearly that at times Jesus performed miracles, not by the Father nor because he as man received supernatural power from the second Person of the Trinity, but because the Holy Spirit had given him the gift to do so. Acts 10:38 indicates this same truth, when Peter speaks of "how God anointed Jesus of Nazareth with the Holy Spirit and power, and how he went around doing good and healing all who were under the power of the devil, because God was with him." Thus the baptism, preaching, and miracles of Jesus show that he entered upon his official ministry not in his own strength but empowered and equipped by the Holy Spirit.

V. His Temptation

Another great work of the Spirit in the life of Christ is revealed in connection with the temptations of Jesus. These all took place under the leadership and guidance of the Holy Spirit.

Right after the baptism, as he was about to be tempted, we read that he was "full of the Holy Spirit." This is probably a reference to the descent of the Spirit at the baptism. Then the Gospels say that he was "led by the Spirit in the desert." Although Matthew and Mark say "into" the desert, Luke says specifically "in" the desert, and he uses a verbal tense, the imperfect, that indicates not a momentary act, but a period of time. The clear indication, therefore, is that the Holy Spirit not only led Christ into the desert, but that all the time Christ was there the Holy Spirit was with him, guiding and helping him to overcome the temptations. And after they were all over, Luke says that he "returned . . . in the power of the Spirit" (4:14). In other words, the whole period of temptation from beginning to end was under the control of the Holy Spirit, and it was by means of the Spirit that Jesus' human nature was given the strength to overcome the severe temptations placed before him. He did not have victory because his divine nature infused divine qualities into his human nature, enabling him to resist. No, for then he would no longer have been man. Instead, being complete man, he relied upon the indwelling of the Spirit for ability to resist evil.

It is safe to assume that Christ needed the Holy Spirit not only during these temptations, but during all the trials of his whole ministry. We know that after these first temptations Satan departed from him only "until an opportune time" (Luke 4:13).

VI. His Death

This amazing Spirit was active from the time of Christ's very conception right down through his death. Hebrews 9:14 tells us this when it says that Christ "through the eternal Spirit offered himself unblemished to God. . . ." The reference here is to the death of Christ.

The Christian owes his salvation not only to the outward death of Jesus, to that external act by which he expired, but also to his inward attitude as he died. God always demands a proper relationship between the heart and the overt act. He is not pleased with mere external conformation to his will, but there must also be a corresponding attitude in the soul. He does not look only on the lips that say "Lord, Lord" or the cups that are clean on the outside, but demands an attitude of perfect love toward him. If Jesus had gone to the cross unwillingly, sullenly, grudgingly, stoically, simply out of a feeling of necessity, and not willingly, with a perfect, ardent zeal, and with faith toward the Father, no atonement could have been made. If Jesus had said, "I hate to go to the cross. I do not want to, but I suppose I have to do my duty," salvation would not have been won. No satisfaction would have been made, and no righteousness would have been available. There would have been neither a passive nor an active obedience, both of which are necessary for salvation.

But, thanks to the Holy Spirit, Jesus offered a perfect sacrifice. He was not forced to die against his will, but did so voluntarily. He went to death, knowing its consequences, but willingly, with a faith in God, and with love, trust, and obedience. His attitude was perfect.

And all of this was made possible by the Holy Spirit, as Hebrews 9:14 indicates by saying that Christ offered himself without blemish to God "through the eternal Spirit." In other words, it was the Holy Spirit who caused Jesus to have the perfect attitude necessary for accomplishing our redemption. Without him he could not have done it. But by the Holy Spirit Jesus went to the cross with an attitude that was perfect, thereby winning redemption for us.

VII. His Resurrection

Nor did the Spirit's work end with the death of Jesus; it continued through his resurrection. Although sometimes the resurrection of Christ is attributed to the Father (Acts 2:24) and sometimes to the Son (John 10:17, 18), yet the Bible gives an indirect hint that the Spirit was also active in a special way in Christ's resurrection. In Romans 8:11b we read that God the Father will give life to our "mortal bodies through his Spirit." If the Father works through the Spirit in the Christian's resurrection, the parallelism established in the Bible between the resurrection of the Christian and that of Christ would suggest that the Spirit also performed a peculiar work in Christ's resurrection.

VIII. His Glorification

The final act of the Holy Spirit in the life of Christ is not demonstrable from a particular text, but is a deduction from many. We know that the believer is made completely holy by the Holy Spirit. We infer also that he is the source of all pure religious life, even of those in a sinless state, such as Adam's. It is the Holy Spirit who dwells within saved man forever, even in heaven. This being the case, the Holy Spirit, who began a work in Christ's human nature and continued it through his resurrection, is surely also dwelling in his glorified human nature, just as he does in all saints.

Conclusion

In conclusion there are three things that should be emphasized. In the first place, we must remember that Jesus Christ was true man. In all the phases of his life his divine nature did not, by virtue of its union with the human nature, cause the human nature to cease to be human. It did not deify the human nature. It did not cause the human nature to think, speak, and act like God. For that would deny the true humanity of Jesus. Rather, Jesus was always complete man as well as complete God, and he is even so today in heaven.

This means that the divine nature did not render the Holy

Spirit unnecessary in Christ's life. Jesus, not as God, but as man, needed the Spirit, as we have seen again and again. As man he needed him in his birth to keep him from sin; in his youth to help him grow in holiness, obedience, and wisdom; in his baptism to equip him for his Messianic office; in his temptations to empower him to resist evil; and in his death to enable him to make the perfect sacrifice. Each time the Scriptures speak of the Holy Spirit as aiding Christ. And to deny this need of Jesus is to do violence to the true humanity of Jesus by attributing to it divine powers that it did not possess.

Secondly, if Christ, the perfect man, who was immaculately conceived and therefore free from the taint of original sin both as to its guilt and corruption, was dependent upon the Holy Spirit, then how much more do we need him! We are not united with the Godhead, and we are by nature totally depraved, inclined to all evil. Contrary to Christ's practice, even after we have been regenerated, we grieve the Holy Spirit and thereby diminish his presence within us. Must we, then, not pray even more for the fullness of the indwelling of the Spirit? If Jesus needed the indwelling Spirit as a boy to give him personal holiness and wisdom so that he might increase in favor with God and man, then how much more do our little children, who are sinful by nature, need the Holy Spirit in order that they may grow up in spiritual beauty and increase in the favor of God! If Christ, who was God and sinless, needed as a man the baptism of the Holy Spirit for his preaching, how much more do sinful preachers of the gospel today need the Spirit in their lives so that their preaching may be "with a demonstration of the Spirit's power"! If Christ, in his temptations, needed the Spirit to overcome them and be victorious, how can we expect to be victorious over sin when we go about never asking for a fuller measure of the Holy Spirit in our lives? If Jesus needed the Holy Spirit in order that he might offer himself up to God and obey him willingly and not grudgingly, then how much more will we need the Holy Spirit to enable us to be willing to do whatever God would have us do! Being ever careful to guard the uniqueness of Christ, we must remember that he is also our example in this life. For he showed us the way of holiness and victory over sin by a Spirit-filled life.

And, finally, we wish to stress that the work of the Holy Spirit did not begin with the application in our lives of the redemption obtained by Christ, but he was operative in the very accomplishing of the redemption itself. By himself Jesus Christ was incapable of working out our redemption. As one having a human nature, he needed the Holy Spirit at his conception and birth, as he grew up, as he was baptized into his official ministry, as he was tempted, as he offered himself up in death, as he was resurrected, and as he was glorified. From his conception to his glorification Jesus Christ needed the Holy Spirit in order to work out redemption for us. We must praise the Holy Spirit not only for applying that work in our lives in regeneration and in sanctification, but also for accomplishing redemption itself in Christ Jesus.

The Holy Spirit
and
Regeneration

7

Up to this point, except for the chapter on the Spirit's illumination, we have considered chiefly the Holy Spirit in the *objective* realm, that is, in the realm that is outside of man. We have studied the Holy Spirit's Person and his work in creation, in common grace, in revelation, and in Jesus. In the next few chapters we will turn to the *subjective* work of the Holy Spirit, that is, his influence in man's life. His initial subjective work, regeneration, is of prime importance to every individual. Without it no man can see the kingdom of God (John 3:3). In order, therefore, to attain eternal happiness, man must know in his own life the regenerating activity of the Holy Spirit. To understand clearly this great work of the Spirit, it is necessary to see the need, the manner, and the results of his regenerating influence.

I. The Need

That a man must experience the regenerating work of the Holy Spirit in order to see the kingdom of God is clear. By himself man can never turn to God. He is totally depraved. His intellect, will, and emotions are corrupt through and through.

As far as his intellect is concerned, man cannot understand God
and his kingdom, even when they are explained in the most lucid
fashion; for sin has darkened his understanding and caused him
spiritually to be totally blind (as was seen in chapter 5). As
far as his will is concerned, he cannot will to obey God, for
"everyone who sins is a slave to sin" (John 8:34); and the
natural mind "does not submit to God's law, nor can it do so"
(Rom. 8:7). And as far as his emotions are concerned, he cannot love God, "because the sinful mind is hostile to God"
(Rom. 8:7).

Hence, unregenerate man is utterly unable to turn to God
and do good. "Can the Ethiopian change his skin, or the leopard
his spots?" (Jer. 13:23). Of course not. That is physically and
naturally impossible. Well then, neither can he who is "accustomed to do evil" do good. This means, therefore, that the
natural man needs the Holy Spirit in his life if he is to become
capable of doing spiritual good.

Furthermore, when Jesus says that man must be born again
(John 3:3), he presupposes that before this occurs man is a
spiritual nonentity. The same is presupposed by Paul when he
calls the Christian a new *creation* in Christ Jesus (II Cor. 5:17).
Up to the time of his spiritual birth or creation, then, man does
not exist spiritually. And as it is a contradiction in terms to speak
of nonexistence begetting or creating, so also it is contradiction to speak of natural man begetting and creating himself
spiritually, so that he enters the kingdom of God. If there is to
be a birth or a creation, then it must be caused by a source
outside of the one to be born or created. There must be a birth
from above by God, and more specifically, by the Holy Spirit.
From this viewpoint, also, the regenerating work of the Holy
Spirit is necessary.

The Bible elsewhere describes man without the Holy Spirit as
being a corpse, completely unable to do anything (Eph. 2:1); or
as the dry bones of a human skeleton scattered throughout a
valley with not an iota of life in them (Ezek. 37). In such a
situation the only one who can help is God, who can and does
make a person alive spiritually (Eph. 2:1). Certainly the dry
bones cannot join themselves with the proper bones, then put on
flesh, and finally give themselves life. That requires the Spirit of
the Lord. And it is equally certain that the corpse of Ephesians
2:1 cannot make any contribution, for it is dead. Thus it is an

absolute impossibility for natural man to turn to God without the Spirit of the living God.

He is spiritually as dead as a soldier on the battlefield who has been lying dead on a pathway for days. Now to make that soldier get up by himself and move out of the pathway is impossible. You can present to him the best logic in the world why he should not lie there, and he will not move. You can yell and boom in his ear, and it will do no good. You can try to whip him or kick him, and he still will not get up out of the way. For the soldier is dead! If he is to move, it will be necessary for God to come into his life and restore him, just as Jesus did with Lazarus, who had already begun to smell with decay (John 11:39).

Exactly the same thing is true in the spiritual realm, where by nature man is so dead that he is spiritually putrid. If that person is dead, you can approach him in ever so many ways, but he will not and cannot respond. You can try both the sugar and the vinegar approach. You can attempt to entice him by sweet promises of the forgiveness of his sins, peace of soul, and eternal happiness; or you can thunder in his ear about the majesty of God, Mount Sinai, and the threats of hell. Or you can sit down with him evening on end, showing him the logic of the gospel. Yet, if the Holy Spirit does not give him spiritual life, he can no more respond to the gospel than can the dead soldier to the reasoning of an American marine, or a blind man to printed instructions, or a deaf person to the radio.

Neither is it of any value to use physical threats. Rome never won a soul to Christ by the use of fire, the sword, the hangman's noose, or the torture rack. One of David Livingstone's first converts was an African chief, Sechele, who, like Rome, thought he could make his tribesmen believe by force. So he suggested one day to Livingstone, "I shall call my head man, and with our whips of rhinoceros hide we will soon make them all believe together." He did not realize that the natural man is dead, and that rhinoceros-hide whips cannot make a man believe, but only the Holy Spirit can. For whips cannot touch the soul, but only man's skin. As Jesus once said: "Do not be afraid of those who kill the body but cannot kill the soul" (Matt. 10:28). Only the Holy Spirit can touch a man's soul and make him alive spiritually.

These various reasons, then, show us man's great need for the regenerating work of the Holy Spirit in his life. This is the only force that can bring forth a new creation and can cause the spiritually dead to become alive so that he can enter the kingdom of God.

II. The Manner

Now let us turn to see *how* the Holy Spirit makes one alive— *how* he regenerates. The first thing we must stress is that the Bible tells us very little about how the Spirit regenerates. It is a matter which God has chosen not to reveal. As Paul said, "Your life is hidden with Christ in God" (Col. 3:3). How Christ is mystically united with the believer is a secret. The union cannot be traced and analyzed. You know that it is there, but you cannot say how it came about. It is like atomic energy, about whose devastating force there is no doubt. A Pacific atoll can be evaporated in one blast. But to explain the ultimate origin of the force in the atoms is beyond man. He can only observe the results.

Or, to use the illustration Jesus used when he was talking with Nicodemus: You can hear the wind, you know it is blowing, you can see the leaves tremble and the trees bend, you feel it in your face—but where it comes from, and where it goes, no one knows. It is invisible. Yet the results are manifest. So it is with the Holy Spirit. The results of his regenerating work are obvious, startling, and plain. But to define his operation in the soul of man defies human ability. One reason, of course, is that both man's soul and the Holy Spirit are spiritual and not material. Therefore, the physical eye cannot discern them. However, certain things that throw some light on his method of operation can be said about the regenerating work of the Holy Spirit.

A. In the first place, regeneration occurs in an instant. It is not a slow, gradual process like the growth of a plant over a period of months or years. A man is either regenerated or he is not. As the Biblical metaphors used to describe regeneration indicate, the Christian is regenerated in a split second. For instance, creation occurs in a moment. Either an object exists or it does not. There is no gradual, in-between stage. A dead man is resurrected in the twinkling of an eye. He is either dead or alive. There is no intermediary stage. A baby is conceived in a moment. There is life, or there is not life. And so regeneration is also instantaneous.

B. In the second place, the Holy Spirit comes and does something to the soul of man. He does not simply present the truths of Christianity to the mind and leave it up to man to accept or reject them. He does not merely approach man in an external manner, trying to persuade him with all kinds of logic and reasoning; but he penetrates into the innermost recesses of man, into his very soul, spirit, or heart (all of which describe the same thing). Regeneration is not simply a change of acts, a reformation of life, a renovation of man's thoughts, words, and deeds. But in regeneration the Holy Spirit touches the spirit of man, which is itself the root of all these actions. He goes to the heart of the matter—the heart of man, the inner core—which is the central, underlying source of all of man's activities.

That man has a center of consciousness—an ego, a heart, a soul—out of which come forth all his thinking and activities is clear from the Bible. For as Proverbs 4:23 says: "Out of the heart are the issues of life." And Christ said: "From within, out of men's hearts, come evil thoughts, sexual immorality, theft, murder, adultery, greed, malice, deceit, lewdness, envy, slander, arrogance and folly. All these evils come from inside . . ." (Mark 7:21-23). Thus the heart is the center of man's being and is the source of all his thinking, willing, emotions, and outward actions of every kind.

So if man's actions and life are to be changed, the source must be changed. If you wish to secure pure water from a spring that is foul, you cannot do so by changing the water after it has left the spring; but it is necessary to get to the source of the matter and change the spring itself. If a person desires beautiful fruit, then he must go to a tree which by nature produces beautiful fruit, for the nature of a tree governs the kind of fruit produced, whether good or bad (Luke 6:43-45). If the fruit that is desired is grapes, then the person must not go to a briar patch, but to a plant that has the nature of a grapevine. There and there alone will he find grapes. Man, too, acts according to his nature. Without the Holy Spirit his nature is corrupt and he brings forth only evil deeds. If he is to do good, then it is not sufficient for another to try to affect him superficially, in an outward fashion, at the periphery, merely presenting truth to his mind. The Spirit must change man's nature, his heart, his innermost core, his inner being. When the heart is good, then all the issues that come forth from that heart will be good, too (cf. Prov. 4:23). Then man can love and praise God, and will to please him.

Accordingly, the Scriptures tell us that God opened Lydia's heart as she listened to Paul preach (Acts 16). Before being thus regenerated, she heard Paul's words but could not understand. It was necessary for the Spirit to regenerate her heart before she could have faith.

Ezekiel also tells us that in order for the Israelites to walk according to God's statutes, their hearts must be changed. God says that he will remove their old, stony hearts, that do not love and obey God, and that he will give them new hearts of flesh, ". . . that they may walk in my statutes, and keep mine ordinances, and do them" (Ezek. 11:20). The nature of the heart governs the nature of the outward actions. In order that the Israelites might walk in God's statutes, God had to give them new hearts.

It is evident, therefore, that in regeneration the Holy Spirit gets at the root of the matter. In some mysterious way he changes the heart or soul of man.

C. However, to describe the work of the Holy Spirit in a third way, this does not mean that the Spirit adds anything new to man's heart, or that he gives it more spirit or new faculties to think or to believe. No, he merely changes its dispositions from love for sin to love for God. When Lazarus was raised from the dead, he was not given new eyes, new ears, or new hands. He had them all already. But he needed life so that he could use them. So Jesus revitalized him.

In a similar fashion, God does not give to man's spiritual nature that is dead in sins and trespasses a new intellect, will, or emotions. Every man, regardless of his depravity, still has these faculties. He has not become a soulless animal. But what is wrong is that these faculties are used for the wrong purpose— for Satan instead of for God. What the Holy Spirit does, therefore, is not to give man an intellect or a will or emotions, but to cause his intellect, will, and emotions to be used *for* God instead of *against* him. He changes the direction of their use.

D. Notice also, that in regeneration the Holy Spirit is absolutely sovereign. He does exactly what he desires. Man cannot frustrate the Spirit, nor control regeneration in any way, for regeneration is not in his hands. As Jesus said, the Holy Spirit is like the wind and "the wind blows wherever it pleases" (John 3:8). No man commands the wind. No one can order a hurricane to blow out to sea instead of toward Florida, or to reduce its speed a little. As Jesus said, it blows where it wills. And so the Holy Spirit regenerates where he wills.

This complete sovereignty of the Spirit in regeneration is also seen from another illustration of Jesus, that of birth. In birth a baby is completely helpless. He does not make himself. He is made. He is born. There is complete passivity on his part. Obviously a baby could not have said to his parents before he was born, "I determine that I shall now be born." And so it is in the case of a spiritual birth. That which is not yet born cannot say, "I will to be born." That which is dead spiritually cannot say, "I will to live." And that which has not yet been created can never say, "I will to be created." These are manifest impossibilities. Rather, as in the case of a baby, or creation yet to be, or a dead man, spiritual birth, creation, or life comes wholly at the discretion of the Holy Spirit. It is he who does the deciding, and not man. Man is entirely passive. The Holy Spirit is entirely sovereign, regenerating exactly whom he wills. Consequently, John could say that the children of God are "born not of natural descent, nor of human decision or a husband's will, but born of God" (John 1:13).

This, incidentally, shows the great error that is so prevalent today in some orthodox Protestant circles, namely, the error that regeneration depends upon faith, and not upon God; and that in order to be born again man must first accept Jesus as his Savior. One pastoral friend states it unequivocally when he says: "We must repudiate the view that God regenerates man before he is convicted of sin, repents, converts, and believes. Such a view makes God arbitrarily determine the salvation or reprobation of individuals on no other principles than his own good pleasure or sovereign will . . . Therefore, rather than saying that conviction, repentance, conversion, and faith come after regeneration, let us hold to the usual Scriptural order, which places regeneration as logically dependent upon these. . . ."

This preacher sees correctly that if regeneration precedes[1]

---

[1] When we speak of regeneration preceding faith, we are not thinking primarily of a time sequence but rather of a causal sequence. Sometimes the two may occur at the same time. But the Bible teaches unequivocally that salvation is entirely of grace—a gift from God. In accord with that, what is being stressed here is that although regeneration and faith may occur

faith, then salvation is entirely in God's hands and according to his own good pleasure and sovereign will. That is precisely what Paul says in Ephesians 1:4, 5, where he writes that God "chose us in him [Christ] before the creation of the world to be holy and blameless in his sight. In love he predestined us to be adopted as sons through Jesus Christ, in accordance with his pleasure and will. . . ." If regeneration does not precede faith, but rather follows and depends upon it, then salvation is of him that runs and of him that wills, but not of God, in direct contradiction to Romans 9:7, which says just the opposite. Then Luke was wrong in saying that God first opened Lydia's heart, and afterward she believed. Then Jesus was mistaken when he asserted that the Holy Spirit is like the wind that blows where it wills, and when he compared the Spirit's work to birth, in which a baby is entirely passive. Then man it not *dead* in his sins and trespasses, for if he is able to believe, he already has spiritual life. And finally, then Paul was in error when he said: "No one can say, 'Jesus is Lord,' except by the Holy Spirit" (I Cor. 12:3).

According to Scripture, faith does not precede and cause regeneration, but rather, regeneration precedes and causes faith. Regeneration is necessary before man can do a single thing that is spiritually good. In regeneration man is 100 percent passive, and the Holy Spirit is 100 percent active.

Thus, although we can say very little about the manner in which the Holy Spirit regenerates, this much we do know. Regeneration occurs instantaneously, in the twinkling of an eye. Further, the Holy Spirit does something to the very soul of man —his heart—and this in turn affects *all* his actions, whether in mind or in deed. The Spirit does not, however, give man a new substance or new faculties, but he revitalizes the soul which he already has. He also acts sovereignly and irresistibly, while man is wholly passive. But even though we know all this, the whole process is still very mysterious to us. We can see neither the wind nor the Holy Spirit.

III. The Results

Although we cannot see the wind, we can see its results. We can see the power it unleashes as a hurricane uproots trees and

---

simultaneously, faith is dependent on regeneration and not vice-versa. Regeneration is necessary for faith, and not the reverse.

carries away homes. Likewise, in regeneration, we may not know how the Holy Spirit operates, but it is possible to see the results, as Jesus' illustration indicates.

For the result is that old sins are going to be put away. New virtues will take their place. Where it was formerly impossible to overcome sins and hate toward God, all is different now, for the Holy Spirit has planted new inclinations and new desires. The bitter spring has been changed to a sweet one, so that the water that flows from it now is sweet. The bramble patch has been changed into a vineyard, so that grapes grow instead of thistles (Luke 6:43-45). The heart of stone has been changed to a heart of flesh, and there is life. A man has been born, the dead has been raised, something new has been created. The old man, in principle, is put off; the new is put on. Jesus sums it up when he says that he that is born again sees the kingdom of God. He has entered in. He has been translated out of the kingdom of darkness into the kingdom of light.

The Holy Spirit's working in regeneration is of tremendous comfort to all who are concerned about the lost. For without the Holy Spirit, no one could be saved. David Livingstone, in one of his darker moments, wrote home: "We have a difficult, difficult field to cultivate here. . . . But for the belief that the Holy Spirit works and will work for us, I should give up in despair." The leopard cannot change his spots, nor the Ethiopian his skin. But God sends his Spirit, and his people are irresistibly converted.

One reason Christians are lax in witnessing to others about Christ is that they often see no results. It is not necessarily that they are ashamed of the gospel of Christ, but it is often that they are discouraged. The lack of positive results makes them wonder whether it is worthwhile. If we are to overcome this, then we will have to pray much more for the regenerating work of the Holy Spirit. For without him none shall be saved.

Jesus said before his death: "It is for your good that I am going away. Unless I go away, the Counselor will not come to you. . . . When he comes, he will prove the world wrong [or *convict the world*, KJV] about sin and righteousness and judgment" (John 16:7, 8). Praise God for that convicting work of the Spirit! It makes a man feel intensely uncomfortable. His conscience bothers him. He becomes restless. Everything seems to be against him. His sins loom before him. His conscience troubles him. He cries. He feels pricked in his heart, as were the three thousand when the Holy Spirit was poured out at Pentecost, and like them he cries: "Brothers, what shall we do?" (Acts 2:37). Then, through this conviction, the man is driven to Christ as the one who made a substitutionary atonement for sin. He repents, believes, and is saved. Through convicting pain he finds joy; through anguish of soul he discovers peace.

And the beauty of it all is that man cannot resist the Spirit's work. When the Holy Spirit convicts, it makes no difference who the person is—how big the brute or how hardened the sinner or whatever his past—the man melts into tears before the Spirit, and his heart is so changed that he has to accept Christ as his Savior. The most calloused sinner who is dead in his sins can never in the most minute fashion resist his being born spiritually by the Holy Spirit. Praise God, he *has* to believe.

If there is one thing that we need today it is the Holy Spirit. If we are to have the peace that passes all understanding, if we are to have any success at all in winning souls to Christ, then the Holy Spirit must come into the lives of the spiritually dead. Therefore, above all, pray for the regenerating influence of the Holy Spirit.

The Holy Spirit and Sanctification 8

In the last chapter we saw that by regeneration the Holy Spirit resurrects dead men—men who are as dead spiritually as the body of a soldier which has been lying on a battlefield for a week. The Holy Spirit gives to dead men spiritual life so that they can perform good deeds, deeds which were impossible when they were dead. This is a great miracle.

There is all the difference in the world between this spiritual life and the death which preceded. However, it is only too evident that this life is often a sickly one. For it is a fact that the Christian still sins. Sometimes he sins so much that it almost looks as if the new life had left him entirely, and he were dead again. But we know that he is not dead. His infirmities will not be unto death, nor are they incurable. On the contrary, these infirmities will gradually disappear. In the meantime, however, there is no doubt that he is really sick.

That the born-again person sins is obvious from his own experience as well as from Scripture. Each Christian is aware only too bitterly of the sinful failures in his life. He may even feel despondent at times because of the seeming victory of sin in his life, and he may exclaim with converted Paul, "What a wretched man I am!" (Rom. 7:24). Humbly he feels the need of the prayer that Christ taught the saved: "Forgive us our sins." John confirms this by remarking that if anyone, including the regenerated, says that he has no sin, he deceives himself, the truth is not in him, and he makes God a liar (I John 1:8, 10).

In fact, the remarkable truth is that the holier and more sanctified a Christian becomes, the greater is his awareness of his own sin. The closer a person is to the holy God, the more sensitive are his feelings for sin. Not only do his gross sins grieve him more, but also, those that before did not trouble him because of their seeming unimportance now loom large in his mind. It was just because Paul had attained such a great degree of sanctification and was thus so sensitive to sin that he complained, "What a wretched man I am!" It was just exactly when Isaiah had a vision of the holy LORD, and when the seraphim cried: "Holy, holy, holy, is the LORD of hosts," that Isaiah said: "Woe is me! for I am undone; because I am a man of unclean lips" (Isa. 6:5). Thus, none are completely holy in this life, not even the greatest saints of God. Regenerated man still sins. Although he has life, it is a sickly one.

This now poses the problem for us: How may we overcome this sin? How may we conquer the anger, temper, hate, envy, sexual lusts, and other evils that well up inside us? Every real Christian is concerned with this. He seeks victory over the sin in his life. How is he to gain it?

The answer the Bible gives to this pressing problem is found in the title of this chapter, "The Holy Spirit and Sanctification." The eternal Spirit of God is the source of sanctification. So that this will be absolutely clear, however, it is necessary, first of all, to observe two solutions that have often been given to this problem of sin, both of which are unbliblical and therefore erroneous. One is essentially: Fight sin all you can. And the other is diametrically the opposite: Do not fight sin. By seeing the error of these two proposed solutions, we shall understand more accurately what the only and victorious solution is: the Biblical answer.

The first proposed answer commands us to rely on our own strength. It leaves sanctification entirely up to us. We are told to control our sinful desires by reason. The advantages of virtue and the sweet promises of the gospel are pointed out. The reasonableness of our duty to God is shown. The consequences of sin to our bodies and souls, both here and in eternity, are cited. Knowing what is good and holy, we are then told: Now, master your life. Conquer all evil tendencies. Exercise all the discipline, determination, resolution, and control that are within you. Follow the example of a man such as Benjamin Franklin, who records in his autobiography how he improved himself by making a daily check list of all his bad habits. If we know what is right, and use our reason and resolution, we can conquer sin by our own strength and power.

A second answer that has been set forth is diametrically the opposite of this first one, and it is equally wrong. If the error of the first-mentioned solution was its assertion that we must fight sin in our own strength, the error of this solution is its belief that we must not fight sin at all, but let Christ do it for us. It is the difference between the mottoes: "Do all" and "Do nothing at all."[1]

Keswick leaders assert, for example, that "deliverance [from sin] is not attained by struggle and painful effort, by earnest resolution and self-denial." If man does anything to defeat sin, sin will defeat him. Man must "simply give God a chance to take hold of the personality. . . . The Holy Spirit wants to free and liberate the personality," but cannot until man lets him.

In this country Hannah Whitall Smith, in *The Christian's Secret of a Happy Life,* stressed that the Christian must surrender completely to the Lord. He must put his life in the Maker's hands like clay in the potter's, and then be passive. "The potter must do all the work." "When we have put our case in the Lord's hands our part is simply to 'sit still.'" "And we must remember this—that if we carry a burden ourselves, the Lord does not carry it."

Trumbull, in his "Victorious Life" movement, urged the motto, "Let go and let God." He said also, "If it isn't easy, it isn't good." "Any victory that you have to get by trying for it is counterfeit. If you have to work for the victory, it is not the real thing." "We must not try not to sin." Such efforts "can and do effectually prevent such victory." When victory is gained it will

---

[1] Although this view in the estimation of the author is not Scriptural, it must be remembered that its proponents have nothing in common with the Modernists of the previous error. On the contrary, they love the infallible Word of God and supernatural Christianity, and their zeal for holiness should be deeply appreciated.

be "victory by freedom rather than victory by fight," "effortless freedom" from all "sinful impulses." "Therefore, stop trying. Let him do it all."

Often in these movements the stress is on the second blessing. It is taught that, just as a man receives Christ in justification without works by faith, so man receives Christ a second time in sanctification by an act of faith that is distinct and separate from the one by which a Christian is justified. They believe that, as in justification the Christian receives Christ instantaneously and completely, so also in sanctification he receives Christ suddenly, in a twinkling of an eye, and not gradually. The difference is that the first time he receives Christ as his personal Savior, and the second time as his Lord who gives him complete victory over all known sin. This is what they call instantaneous, sinless perfection by the second blessing.

Both of these proposed solutions to victory over sin are unbiblical. Man will never find holiness only by striving with might and main in his own strength. Something else is needed—supernatural help. Neither will man gain the victory by simply relying on supernatural help without striving with all that is within him. But victory over sin may and can be had by what might superficially seem to be a combination of these two. The secret to holiness, according to the Bible, is to be found in a twofold activity: God's working in us and our working, too. This is the way of victory for the Christian.

The first thing necessary for conquering the power of sin in our lives is the regenerating work of the Holy Spirit. Because the Spirit is working in our lives, Jesus Christ comes to live in our hearts. We become mystically united with him. This is not a union by memory, nor by some feeling, nor by love as might exist between two friends. But in an ontological way Christ comes and dwells within our lives and is united with us. The union is just as real as, although not identical to, the union of branches to their vine (John 15:5), or of the Son to the Father in the Trinity (John 17:21), or of the head to the body (Eph. 4:16, 17). It is of such reality that Paul can say: "I have been crucified with Christ and I no longer live, but Christ lives in me" (Gal. 2:20).

When the Spirit thus regenerates, and a union is established with Christ, then victory over sin follows—a victory which is instantaneous and not gradual. To be sure, there is not a complete eradication of sin in the Christian on earth, yet there is a victory that is secured in a moment, so that John can write, "This is the victory that has overcome the world" (I John 5:4). And Paul can declare emphatically, "For sin shall not be your master" (Rom. 6:14). Sin is conquered. The sinner is victorious. Of course, he will continue to sin (I John 1:8), but it will be against his will, so that "it is no longer I myself who do it, but it is sin living in me" (Rom. 7:17). It may seem at times that he has no hope and is more the victim of sin than the victor over it. Yet, he who is born of the Spirit and united to Christ cannot abandon himself to sin. For he is dead to sin, and sin shall not have dominion over him. Sin may conquer temporarily and in different ways, but ultimately it shall be completely eradicated in every way. Satan has been given a mortal blow—he is doomed. But in the meantime he goes down fighting.

The victory may be compared to the Allied victory over the Japanese in 1945. Victory was won. The Japanese surrendered. The fighting was over. But even after the peace treaty had been signed and the bulk of the Japanese army had capitulated, there were some who kept on fighting when Americans attempted to occupy the islands. Similarly in the life of everyone who is mystically united with Christ Jesus, the victory has been won. Satan and sin are defeated. It has already happened. There is still guerrilla warfare carried on sporadically, and at times it takes on great proportions, but the victory is sealed, and it is only a matter of time before the last vestige of opposition (sin) will be done away with. In this Biblical sense, it is possible to speak of the victorious life (I John 5:4).

It is not easy to characterize the actual sanctifying work of the Holy Spirit. It is a mystery, just like regeneration, and yet a few things can be said about it.

In the first place, sanctification is primarily the work of the Spirit. Although it is true, as we mentioned, that spiritual life comes from being mystically united to Jesus Christ; and although Jesus said in John 14:23 that not only the Holy Spirit dwells in the believer, but also the Father and the Son; and although we know we may not divide the work of the Trinity; yet the Scriptures do indicate that sanctification is chiefly the work of the third Person of the Trinity. He is the one who regenerates (John 3), renews (Titus 3:5), sanctifies (II Thess. 2:13; I Peter 1:2), leads (Rom. 8:14), dwells within man (John 14:17; Rom. 8:9; I Cor. 3:16), and writes on his heart (II Cor. 3:3). And Paul says clearly that "if anyone does not have the Spirit of Christ, he does not belong to Christ" (Rom. 8:9). These passages indicate that the Spirit is absolutely essential for this victorious life in Christ. He who lacks the Spirit does not belong to Christ—does not partake of his life. Hence, if Christ is to sanctify man by dwelling in him, he must do it through the Spirit. Christ and the Father do not indwell and thereby sanctify man directly or immediately, but through the indwelling of the Holy Spirit. In short, sanctification is principally the work of the third Person of the Trinity.

The second characteristic of this sanctifying work is that the Spirit, just as in regeneration, affects the very heart or soul of man. He does not merely use moral, rational persuasion, leaving it to man to sanctify himself or not; but he continually affects his basic nature, touching man in his subconscious life, in the inmost recesses of his soul, where man can neither cooperate nor resist. The result is that good works follow, for the fruit of the tree is governed by its nature, and out of the heart are all the issues of life (Prov. 4:23).

David saw that the Holy Spirit must touch his heart or soul. After his twofold crime of murder and adultery, he pleads for forgiveness. But he wants more than forgiveness: he wants the root of all his sin changed. If God should forgive, and if his heart should remain the same, then the same sins would appear again. So, in addition to asking for forgiveness, he pleads to God, "Create in me a clean heart, O God; and renew a right spirit within me" (Ps. 51:10). Only with a clean heart touched by God will he be able to make progress in avoiding future sins, for, as Christ said, out of the heart of man proceed murder and adulteries.

Thanks be to God that in sanctification the Spirit does operate in that subconscious area of our souls where we cannot resist. Otherwise, we would never be sanctified, for apart from the Spirit we would always resist.

Thirdly, the Holy Spirit causes the *whole* of man to be affected in sanctification. He does not sanctify only the will, for example, so that the Christian determines to do the good, but does not understand the good, or love the good. Rather, he sanctifies *all* of man: his will, his emotions, and his understanding. He does not give a *complete* sanctification at the new birth, but it is a sanctification that affects all of man and starts him on the way of holiness in his entire being. It is similar to the birth and growth of a baby that is perfectly created. The baby has all of the faculties of the mind and body, even though small. His fingernails may be tiny, yet they are perfectly made. He has the right number of fingers, toes, ears, eyebrows, and internal organs, even if they are not fully developed. In a similar fashion, the Holy Spirit regenerates and sanctifies the entirety of man. It may be just a beginning, but every portion of man is affected. His spiritual understanding does not develop to the neglect of his will, nor his will to the detriment of his emotions. But he grows in all parts. He is perfect in parts, but imperfect in degree.

This comprehensiveness of the Spirit's work is derived from such passages as Proverbs 4:23, which tell us that the heart governs all the activities of man, and Mark 7:20-23, where Jesus enumerates the wickednesses, that proceed out of the heart. If the innermost being of man, his heart or soul, is changed, then all of its products and effusions will be altered, too. This is also seen from the various places in the Bible which specifically mention the will, the intellect, and the emotions as being sanctified.

A fourth characteristic of the Spirit's work in sanctification is the *gradualness* of the process. Man never attains instantaneous, sinless perfection on earth. Only if man lowers the standards of God to meet his sinfulness, can he erroneously think that he is perfect. For the Bible testifies that man is not suddenly emancipated from the power of sin, but rather that deliverance comes after a long struggle. Sometimes the process is slow, and at other times it is accelerated, but in any case it is over a period of time. As we have seen, John says that "if we claim to be without sin, we deceive ourselves and the truth is not in us" (I John 1:8). Paul continually speaks about the sin that is still in the Christian, and the incessant warfare with Satan. And Peter does not say, "Jump into grace and knowledge," but rather, *"Grow* in the grace and knowledge of our Lord and Savior Jesus Christ" (II Peter 3:18). This indicates definitely that sanctification is a gradual process.

But, fifth, that gradual process will be completed in the twinkling of an eye at the moment of death. In heaven, in the presence of the holy God, there will be no sin, for sin will have been completely done away (Rev. 21:27). Therefore, when the Christian goes to heaven immediately at death, as the Bible indicates, the process of sanctification is suddenly brought to completion, and in a split second he becomes sinlessly perfect.

This continual operation of the Holy Spirit whereby we are united to Christ is, then, the indispensable condition for victory over our sins, even though that victory is not easy. The indwelling presence of the Spirit and Christ is essential and basic. There is no other way. Without them no victory will be attained—not even a partial one. Firm resolution, determination, and painful striving without the Spirit and Christ are of no avail. For anyone so to attempt such a victory would be like a person trying to produce beautiful, red, juicy apples by gluing seeds or small apples on a tree, and then hoping that they will grow. Such externality will not succeed. Rather, he must select a tree that has a correct nature, the nature of an apple tree. When that is done and proper cultivation is given, that tree will naturally and easily produce good apples. As Christ said: "I am the vine; you are the branches. If a man remains in me and I in him, he will bear much fruit; apart from me you can do nothing" (John 15:5). As branches are united with a vine, and receive from it the life and vitality to grow and produce grapes, so also the Christian dwells in Christ, and from him and the Holy Spirit receives the inward power and life and strength to do good works. And as it is absolutely impossible to produce grapes from an old, dry, dead stick, so also it is impossible to become holy if Christ and the Holy Spirit are not within us giving us life. We receive from Christ the power to overcome sin—power which we do not have in ourselves.

Or to attempt to conquer sin by external means, such as asceticism or discipline or moral persuasion or Benjamin Franklin's check list, in our own strength and without the Spirit, is like trying to make a seedling into a mighty oak by stretching the bark, pulling the limbs, and lifting the trunk. It cannot be forced in that outward fashion.

The Biblical way is illustrated by that same oak in springtime. Dead, dry, brittle, brown leaves are still on some of its branches. As life manifests itself from within, those old leaves naturally fall off, and new, green leaves appear, small at the start, but perfectly formed, and gradually developing into full maturity. In a similar fashion, when the Spirit and Christ dwell within us, they give us such power and life that the old sins drop off one by one, and in their place come new virtues—small, to be sure—but growing gradually and certainly.

Thus, sanctification is not accomplished by externalities—by a great expenditure of determination and will power, apart from an inward source of power. But through the Holy Spirit and Jesus Christ reigning within us, we will find power that the non-Christian does not have, divine power itself. As Jesus said, "Streams of living water will flow from within him" (John 7:38). Herein lies the secret of power and victory—the way of success.

We must now guard ourselves against a possible error. Perhaps someone will say that since victory is attained only by the Holy Spirit, we must leave it all to him. We should not work as hard as we can to overcome sin. As some have said, we should "let Him do it all." We should let Christ take over our personality, and we ourselves should just "sit still." "We must not try not to sin," for that will lead to defeat. We must gain an effortless victory, in which we are absolutely passive.

This teaching is not Biblical, and it is dangerous. It is true that without Christ and the Spirit no victory is possible. They must dwell within our bodies. But at the same time, the whole of Scripture clamors for action on our part. The work of the Holy Spirit does not make our activity unnecessary.

In regeneration the Christian is only passive. He can do nothing about it. He is simply born: he does not cooperate in his birth. Just like a baby, he contributes nothing to it. But in sanctification there is an additional aspect. Man is both passive and active. To be sure, it is the Holy Spirit who sovereignly works within his life in his subconscious area, in his heart, so that man is absolutely passive in this operation. Man does not control the Spirit or Christ, but their life flows to him apart from his activity. He is utterly passive in this side of sanctification.

Yet at the same time, man is very active, not in the reception of spiritual life, but in the working out of that life which the Holy Spirit gives to him. He is not treated like a clock that we wind up tightly and then set on a table to tick and run by itself. For man has a will, emotions, and an intellect, which a clock does not have. When the Holy Spirit sanctifies man, he has respect for these faculties, using them, and causing them to move into action. Accordingly, sanctification is both a passive and an active work. It is both a grace and a duty: a grace in which the

Spirit is sovereignly bestowed upon those who passively receive him, and a duty whereby, once the Spirit is received, the recipients are called to action.

To be sure, we do not act in our own power, but only in so far as the Spirit graciously gives us power and ability to act. It is not as though the Spirit works partially in us, setting us in motion, whereupon we do the rest. Rather, God works 100 percent in all we do, and we work 100 percent in all we do. It is because the Spirit works in us that we are able to work. Every single ethical act we do—whether it is resisting temptation, doing a positive good, or believing on Jesus Christ—we do only because the Spirit enables us to do it. Yet, true as this may be, it is our solemn obligation to try as hard as we can. We may not "sit still," "let Him do it all," and seek an "effortless victory." The Bible teaches: If it isn't hard, it isn't good.

Although victory is found only through the Spirit and Christ, nevertheless the Scriptures constantly encourage us to join the fight against sin and the devil. They say: "Fight the good fight of the faith" (I Tim. 6:12); "Put on the full armor of God so that you can take your stand against the devil's schemes. For our struggle is not against flesh and blood . . ." (Eph. 6:11, 12); "Therefore, I urge you, brothers, in view of God's mercy, to offer yourselves as living sacrifices, holy and pleasing to God. . . . Do not be conformed any longer to the pattern of this world, but be transformed . . ." (Rom. 12:1, 2); "Let us purify ourselves" (II Cor. 7:1); "Therefore . . . let us throw off everything that hinders . . . and let us run with perseverance the race marked out for us" (Heb. 12:1); and, "Run in such a way to get the prize" (I Cor. 9:24). It would be possible to go on in endless repetition, citing Scripture after Scripture which exhorts the Christian to strive to be perfect even as his Father in heaven is perfect. All these Scripture passages point to the fact that *the Christian* must act, *he* must do something. In other words, there is a very active side to sanctification.

Perhaps no passage shows the relationship of the active and passive side in a finer way than Philippians 2:12, 13. Here Paul does not say: Sit still; be passive as clay in the potter's hand; do nothing; do not try; just let the Spirit do it all. On the contrary, he emphatically and unambiguously says: "Work!" "Continue to work out your salvation with fear and trembling." This refers to the active side of sanctification, to man's duty and responsibility. Paul exhorts the Philippians to put forth every effort they can to become holy. They may not say: Leave it to God; he will do it all; we will not work. Rather, Paul commands that they make work of it.

But the passive side immediately follows, when Paul adds, "For it is God who works in you to will and to act according to his good purpose." Yes, work! Work with all you have; work with all that is in you. It is your responsibility. But, remember! it is God who is working in you to will and to act.

There is the Biblical combination, and that is the magic to success. If one part is attempted without the other, failure will result. If we work without the Spirit, we will be frustrated. On the other hand, if we leave it all to the Spirit and do not work, we will also end in failure. But combine the Spirit with work; then increasing victory will be ours. The secret of holy living is found in this combination. With it the Christian can have success.

Without attempting to be complete, we would like to suggest three concrete and practical steps which the Christian can take (entirely by the Spirit's grace, of course) and which will help him to hasten the final victory.

The first work is to pray for a fuller presence of the Holy Spirit and Christ in his life. Although it is true that the Spirit causes us to pray in faith for himself and Christ, it is a Biblical axiom that the more we seek by faith their indwelling presence, the more they will come into our lives. For faith is the means of appropriating the Spirit and Christ, just as the hand is the means by which we appropriate physical bread for our bodies. Jesus said: "Whoever believes in me, as the Scripture has said, streams of living water will flow from within him. By this he meant the Spirit, whom those who believed in him were later to receive" (John 7:38, 39). Paul prayed for the Ephesians, that "Christ may dwell in your hearts through faith" (Eph. 3:17). To the Galatians he declared that Christ dwelled within himself, and that he lived that Christ-indwelt life by faith (Gal. 2:20). Thus, faith is the key to the fuller indwelling of the Holy Spirit and Christ, and, consequently, to the receiving of power over sin. We may pray in faith for an increased indwelling of the Spirit in our lives, and we shall receive it.

We must remember that prayer is not simply a pious expression of devotion and thanks to God, but it is also a means of power.

It is always requisite, however, to pray aright. It is necessary to persevere, for example—to go to God again and again with the same request. It is also essential to go believing and expecting that he will answer our prayers, and not simply desiring an answer, thinking at the same time that God will not grant it. That is not faith. Faith is composed of trust as well as of knowledge. We must not only know that God is able to give us a greater indwelling of the Spirit and Christ; we must also trust that he will do so. When we go in this expectation and trust, we will find that God, who loves to bestow his good and holy gifts, will give us a fuller indwelling. This will mean, in turn, that we will have greater victory over sin. The first and the prime work, therefore, that we can do to overcome sin is to pray in faith for the indwelling presence of Christ and the Holy Spirit.

A second important means which we must lay hold of if we are to have victory is private meditation on the Word of God. Except in the case of infants, the Holy Spirit does not work apart from the Word of God. He works *through* that Word. How can we expect to be holy and to do God's will if we neglect the God-given means of grace and rarely read the only Book which shows us what holiness is? In the Bible we see our holy example, Jesus Christ. We find written instructions, either explicit or implicit, for our own lives. If we are to be conformed to the image of the Son, then we must be intimately acquainted with him in the Bible. If we are to keep all of God's precepts, as they are given on every page of the Bible, then we must read them. We cannot lazily hope that the Spirit will miraculously reveal them to us by another revelation. No, we must be saturated with that Word, for the Spirit works through it. As we feed on that Word, the Spirit will work within us, causing us to be increasingly sanctified. Jesus clearly taught that we are sanctified by the truth (John 17:17, 19). Peter confirmed this when he said: "Crave pure spiritual milk, so that by it you may grow up in your salvation" (I Peter 2:2). A second concrete work, then, which will enable us to conquer the sin remaining within us is thorough, personal meditation on the Word.

Finally, the Christian seeking a holier life will be faithful in public worship. Through the faithful, official preaching of the Word, the Holy Spirit will speak, convict him of sin, and lead him to holiness. In the sacraments, he will also find his faith being strengthened.

Suppose, for example, that as a pastor preached on sanctification, some of his parishioners who were struggling with certain sins had not come to church, but had stayed home. They would then have missed this official proclamation of the Word of God on their very problem, and they would not have grown as much as they could have. The Holy Spirit works through the official exposition of the Word. Thus the Christian who desires to be holy will be diligent in attending all worship services.

Along these paths the Bible directs us toward victory over sin—over any sin that may be in our lives, whether it be anger, impatience, hate, envy, sexual lust, drunkenness, lack of love toward God, or any other sin. Sanctification is a twofold work. First of all, it is 100 percent the work of God. We must experience, through his sovereign grace, the indwelling of the Holy Spirit. Without him we can do absolutely nothing: we are doomed to defeat. With him we can do all things. We have a source of divine power that can conquer sin.

Second, sanctification is accomplished by the persistent and determined work of man. He must, by the grace of God, strive to the utmost for perfection.

Couple these two elements—God's work and man's work—and the outcome is victory over sin. To be sure, on this side of death sin will not be eradicated. But there will be a marked and definite progress toward complete sanctification, and on the other side of death it will be perfected.

This is the secret to the Biblical "Higher Life": this is the "Victorious Life."

The Holy Spirit and Tongue-Speaking

9

Tongue-speaking is the spontaneous speaking in a language that has not been previously learned by the speaker, or in syllables that are not recognized as a language.

Speaking in tongues occurred in the New Testament days and then went into oblivion for at least eighteen hundred years—if not permanently. Some say that the second-century Montanists spoke in tongues, but few want to claim a Biblical basis for the raving, ecstatic utterances of this non-Christian sect.[1] The church fathers did not practice, nor did they refer to, tongue-speaking in their day.[2] By the fourth century, Chrysostom in the Eastern church and Augustine in the Western church found glossolalia a thing of the past. In the Middle Ages there are some

---

[1] Ecstatic tongue-speaking is found not only among Christians, but also among many non-Christians, such as the Eskimos, Zulus, Hindus, Moslems, and Mormons. Thus glossolalia is not necessarily the result of the working of the Holy Spirit.

[2] Some think Irenaeus (died A.D. 200) spoke about tongue-speaking, but see Anthony Hoekema's *What About Tongue-Speaking?* (Eerdmans, 1966), pp. 12-15. This is one of the finest introductions into glossolalia that is available. An excellent, more thorough study is Dale Bruner's *A Theology of the Holy Spirit* (Eerdmans, 1970).

infrequent reports of speaking in a foreign language. None of the Reformers—Luther, Calvin, Zwingli, Knox, Melancthon— spoke in tongues. Apart from a few scattered instances of tongue-speaking in the Middle Ages and post-Reformational days, so-called tongue-speaking was not revived until the turn of this century. Thus there was a silence of tongues for eighteen hundred years, and many say that the silence still continues and that what is called tongue-speaking today has little to do with the Biblical concept.

Today tongue-speaking is usually associated with what is called the second blessing or the baptism in (or *of* or *with*) the Holy Spirit. It is believed by many that a person accepts Christ as his Savior from the guilt of his sins, and that at some subsequent time the Holy Spirit rushes on him suddenly, so that he is filled with the Spirit. As a sinner he accepts Christ, but as a saint he accepts the Holy Spirit. In the one case he puts his faith in Christ; in the other case, in the Spirit. As an evidence of this filling, they say, God gives the gift of glossolalia (tongue-speaking). It can be used for self-edification as well as for congregational uplifting. Both the baptism in the Spirit and the accompanying glossolalia are obtained by an intense longing for the Spirit's baptism by prayer, and by a removal of all known sin.

Since tongue-speaking is a widespread practice today—cutting across denominations—it is important for the Christian to study what the New Testament says about it. For he cannot escape it. He should know what is Biblical. Is he missing something beautiful and edifying if he does not speak in tongues? Is there really a spiritual gift today of tongue-speaking or is this a hallucination or a movement from the devil? Did tongue-speaking cease with the end of the New Testament era? Is there an instantaneous second blessing to be obtained by a sudden filling of the Holy Spirit? Can one become a better Christian by the Spirit's baptism and glossolalia? Will these help one's drab Christian life that often seems so sinful?

I. Tongue-speaking in the Apostolic Era

There is much evidence in the Bible that tongue-speaking was confined to the apostolic era, since it was for the purpose of confirming to the Gentiles and Jews God's dramatically new work in Christ Jesus. Yet some believe that the evidence is not conclusive. Let us look at some of the data.

A. *Acts 14:3.* On their first missionary journey, Paul and Barnabas encountered great opposition in Iconium. In fact, both Jews and Gentiles plotted against them and were planning on stoning them to death. In the face of such animated hostility to the message of Christ, which seemed so radically new to both the Jews and Gentiles, God worked signs and miracles through the apostles. As Luke says: "Paul and Barnabas spent considerable time there, speaking boldly for the Lord, who confirmed the message of his grace by enabling them to do miraculous signs and wonders" (Acts 14:3). Speaking in tongues is not mentioned here, nor are other signs. And maybe there was no tongue-speaking in Iconium, but tongues were sometimes given as a sign (I Cor. 14:22), and Luke is clear in telling us that the purpose of the signs was to confirm the message of Paul and Barnabas.

B. *Romans 15:18-19.* Paul develops a similar theme in this passage, when he writes: "I will not venture to speak of anything except what Christ has accomplished through me in leading the Gentiles to obey God by what I have said and done— by the power of signs and miracles, through the power of the Holy Spirit." Interestingly, Paul mentions three instruments of conversion: (1) The Holy Spirit, (2) Paul's preaching and deeds, and (3) the signs and miracles. In harmony with what Luke says in Acts 14, Paul here states that Christ uses signs (glossolalia could be included in signs) to cause the Gentiles to obey God. The purpose of the signs was for conversion.

C. *II Corinthians 12:12.* In II Corinthians Paul constantly defends his apostleship, and in 12:11 he says: "I am not the least inferior to the 'super-apostles,' even though I am nothing." Then to give proof that he was an apostle he says in the next verse: "The things that mark an apostle—signs, wonders and miracles—were done among you with great perseverance." In other words, signs were given to prove apostleship.

D. *Hebrews 2:3-4.* "This salvation, which was first announced by the Lord, was confirmed to us by those who heard him. God also testified to it by signs, wonders and various miracles, and gifts of the Holy Spirit distributed according to his will." Here the author clearly speaks of the confirming nature of signs. He says that first Christ announced salvation. Then those who listened to him confirmed it to others. And finally God added his testimony in the form of signs.

E. *John 20:30-31.* Although Jesus never spoke in tongues, his use of signs fits in with this purpose of confirming the gospel. John writes: "Jesus did many other miraculous signs in the presence of his disciples, which are not recorded in this book. But these are written that you may believe that Jesus is the Christ, the Son of God, and that by believing you may have life in his name."

Thus, on the basis of such passages as these, many assert that tongue-speaking was a sign of the apostolic age, granted by God in order to authenticate and confirm the gospel—and those who preached it—as it spread out beyond the millennia-old boundary of Judaism into the Gentile world. It was his stamp of approval on the gospel and was designed to win converts in this difficult and radically different new period. Once this confirmation was made, they say, there was no longer a need for the special office of apostles or prophets or the confirmatory signs—such as tongue-speaking—that accompanied their work. So with the New Testament church firmly established, the special offices and signs ceased. This viewpoint is very attractive.

II. The Biblical Perspective on the Importance of Tongue-speaking

Some argue that God is not bound and can still perform signs, including tongue-speaking.[3] We must not restrict the freedom of the Holy Spirit.

It is certainly possible that God is working today through miraculous signs, including tongue-speaking. It may be that there are genuine miraculous healings, although many observers feel that their number is greatly exaggerated. There are too many cases of "healed" people who died of their ailment a short while later, when they should have gone to the God-given doctors rather than to the misleading faith healers.

So, without affirming or denying the continuation of miracles

[3] This is the conclusion of the sober, lengthy (95 pages) and very useful report submitted to the Christian Reformed Church synod of 1973 (Grand Rapids, 1973). Unfortunately, it did not wrestle at great length with the matter of the cessation of the special gifts and has limited value at this point.

and tongue-speaking in the present age, and presupposing for a moment that they still do occur, the Biblically oriented Christian will want to put them in their right perspective. And the Biblical perspective is this: *Nowhere does the Bible emphasize the importance or desirability of speaking in tongues, and in the one and only passage where the Bible gives us directives about it, it is played down.* In other words, even if the gift of glossolalia is operative today, the Bible does not single it out as a great experience that all should strive for or that is even normal in the Christian life. And the Christian's goal should be to give only as much importance to it as the Bible does—no more and no less. Consider then the evidence:

A. *The Old Testament.* There is no mention of tongue-speaking at all in the Old Testament—not even in the prophetic passages that point to Pentecost. The Old Testament deals with prophecy, healings, miracles, and the work of the Holy Spirit in creation, common grace, revelation, illumination, Jesus Christ, regeneration, sanctification, and prayer. But nowhere does it even hint at glossolalia.[4]

B. *Jesus Christ.* Not once in all the instruction of Jesus is there even a casual mention of tongue-speaking. Nor did he, to whom God gave the Spirit "without limit" (John 4:34), practice it. Jesus tells us the important matters of life: faith, salvation, sanctification, illumination, prayer, obedience, and divine rules for living. But never once does he consider the speaking in tongues important enough to mention it. He gives all kinds of instructions, commands, and examples, but glossolalia is not among them. It will be a bold person who, in contrast to Jesus, will find tongue-speaking to be the next most important experience after having been saved.

Some appeal to Mark 16:17-18 as a passage where Jesus dealt with tongue-speaking: "And these signs will accompany those who believe: In my name they will drive out demons; they will speak in new tongues; they will pick up snakes with their hands; and when they drink deadly poison, it will not hurt them at all; they will place their hands on sick people, and they will get well." But such an appeal is not felicitous:

1. It is the near unanimous consent of all Biblical scholars

---

[4] Isaiah 28:11, 12 does not refer to glossolalia but to the speaking in a foreign language by the Assyrians invading Israel.

—conservative and liberal alike—that Mark 16:9-20 was not inspired by the Holy Spirit but was added later on to God's holy Word. The judgment of the great orthodox stalwart, Benjamin Warfield, is as true today as it was in 1918 when even then he wrote: "Nevertheless it is just as certain that it [Mark 16:17-18] is spurious as anything of this kind can be certain" (*Counterfeit Miracles,* N.Y., p. 167). And today's Bible versions with one accord agree in this judgment. For example, the New International Version separates verses 8 and 9 with a space and a line and then has a note right in the text that reads: "The most reliable early MSS omit Mark 16:17-18." Similarly, The New American Standard Version puts verses 9-20 in brackets (not mere parentheses) and adds this note: "Some of the oldest MSS omit from verse 9 through 20." Other modern versions that treat it similarly are the New English Bible, Revised Standard Version, Berkley, Barclay, and Beck. The two modern Catholic Bibles, restricted by church decisions, state that although this passage is in the canon, it was not written by Mark.

2. If these verses are part of the original Bible and were spoken by Jesus, then it is arbitrary for those who emphasize glossolalia to select one element of Jesus' teaching and neglect the others, such as drinking deadly poison and handling snakes. These two practices are placed right between tongue-speaking and healing. If one is to be practiced, so should they all.

3. But suppose it is granted for a moment that Mark 16:17 was inspired by the Holy Spirit. Then there is still only one place in all of Scripture where Jesus mentions tongue-speaking. And at that, it is no command—only a prediction that it will be practiced. This incidental, single reference would still show that Jesus did not consider it to be very important. If he did, as in the case of faith, love, obedience, and prayer, he would have taught about it at length and would have done it himself.

C. *The Gospels.* Neither do any of the four Gospels cite an example of speaking in tongues or record any of the apostles as giving instructions about it. Thus over a third of the New Testament is completely silent on the matter.

D. *Pentecost.* In Acts, tongue-speaking is mentioned only three times: Acts 2 (Pentecost), Acts 10, 11 (Cornelius), and Acts 19 (Ephesus). In first looking at Pentecost, it should be noted that the tongue-speaking of Pentecost was not the same kind of tongue-speaking that Paul speaks about in I Corinthians 12—14.

1. At Pentecost the apostles spoke in foreign languages to the people who had come from many foreign countries. Interpreters were not needed. But in the case of the ecstatic speaking of I Corinthians 12—14, Paul says that no one could understand the speaking unless it was interpreted for them. This is similar to most tongue-speaking today, which is not done in a foreign language, and is unlike the Pentecostal glossolalia.

2. At Pentecost the ability to communicate in a foreign language came at the transition from the Old Testament to the New Testament. But in the Corinthian church tongue-speaking came to a church that was well beyond this transition.

3. At Pentecost it came once as an initiatory experience, but in Corinth it was a continuing gift.

4. At Pentecost everyone present spoke in tongues, but at Corinth only some had the gift.

5. A final difference is that at Pentecost the ability to speak in foreign languages was granted in order to confirm and authenticate the dramatic outpouring of the Holy Spirit, whereas at Corinth the speaking in tongues was primarily for the edification of self and the church.

For these reasons it is not possible to appeal to the Pentecostal experience of speaking as a basis for either the Corinthian or modern-day tongue-speaking. They are radically different.

E. *Acts 10, 11.* In this passage Luke records how in the early church, not too long after Pentecost, the gospel was extended to a Gentile, Cornelius, a centurion in the Italian regiment. The result of Peter's visit to Cornelius was that the Holy Spirit came on all the Gentiles who heard him, and they all spoke in tongues. This phenomenon of tongue-speaking is not of the same nature as the so-called tongue-speaking of today. Note the differences:

1. In Acts 10 the Holy Spirit came on all and they all talked in tongues. In the case of Corinth or today, only a few in the churches speak in tongues.

2. In Acts 10 there was no long searching for the Spirit or intense desire for him, as is usually demanded by glossolalists today. There were no conditions that had to be fulfilled. Rather, as Peter explained the gospel for the first time, the Spirit came

on them and they talked in tongues. It was God's dramatic gift and not the result of man's effort.

3. In the case of Cornelius the special gifts of the Holy Spirit and glossolalia came only on those who were accepting Christ for the first time and who had not even been baptized. They did not come on Peter and the six men who came with him and who were already believers. In the modern movement it is claimed that the Holy Spirit and glossolalia comes only on believers some time after they have been saved. But here faith, the descent of the Spirit, and glossolalia were simultaneous. As soon as Cornelius and his household believed, the Spirit came on them and they all spoke in tongues. After that, they were baptized as a sign that they had been regenerated (11:18).

In this passage God is primarily telling us that the gospel is not only for the Jews but also for the Gentiles. That was the purpose of Peter's vision, in which God commanded him to eat the food that came down in a sheet from heaven, even though for centuries the food had been forbidden by Jewish law. For the Jews, who for two thousand years had been accustomed to thinking that they were God's chosen ones and that the Gentiles were anathema to God, it was hard to believe that God had changed his ways. So as a confirmation of that fact, God acted dramatically at both Pentecost and Cornelius's home. Peter said: "The Holy Spirit came on them as he had come on us at the beginning" (11:15), meaning at Pentecost. On these Gentiles who believed for the first time, God sent the sign of tongue-speaking to confirm that the Spirit had indeed been given to them. It was this external evidence that convinced Jewish believers in the church at Jerusalem so that they said: "So, then, God has even granted the Gentiles repentance unto life" (11:18).

F. *Acts 19:1-17.* This passage tells of Paul's visit to the Gentiles at Ephesus: How the Ephesians had been baptized with John's baptism, but now through Paul's ministry were baptized into Christ; how the Holy Spirit came on them; and how they spoke in tongues and prophesied.

The events at Ephesus are very similar to those around Cornelius and have little to do with modern glossolalia:

1. The gift of tongues came on Gentiles.

2. It came on all—not just a few.

3. It was simultaneous with their believing, and not subsequent as a second blessing.

4. There was no fulfillment of certain conditions other than the one Biblical demand of repentance of sin and faith in Christ.

5. Its purpose was to confirm God's action in extending the gospel to the Gentiles. The Ephesians had been baptized with John's baptism. But now that Christ had died, now that the Spirit had come at Pentecost, it was important that they be rebaptized, this time into Christ. And as a sign of God's good pleasure in this dramatic shift from Jew to Gentile, God grants the outpouring of the Spirit and its external manifestations in tongue-speaking and prophesying to these Gentile Ephesians.

Thus, in summarizing the three places in Acts that deal with tongue-speaking, we find that this gift is not the same as tongue-speaking today. Today it is a coveted sign that comes sometime after one accepts Christ as Savior, that comes on only a few, and whose purpose is the edification of the speaker or others in the church. But in the days of Acts, tongue-speaking came without being sought, at the time of conversion, on all, and for the purpose of showing God's good pleasure in extending the gospel to the Gentile. So again we find little Biblical support for tongue-speaking.[5]

G. *I Cor. 12—14.* The great passage on tongue-speaking is Paul's three-chapter discussion in I Corinthians. This is the only passage in the Bible that deals with the tongue-speaking that is for edification and that is similar to the modern glossolalia movement.[6] The remarkable thing to note is that in this solitary Pauline passage on glossolalia, Paul does not elevate tongue-

---

[5] It should also be noted that nine times Acts speaks of people being filled with the Holy Spirit and yet there is no evidence that as a result they spoke in tongues: Peter (4:8), believers (4:31), the seven (6:3), Stephen (6:5; 7:55), Paul (9:17; 13:9), Barnabas (11:24) and disciples at Antioch (13:52).

[6] Some believe that the tongue-speaking of I Cor. 12—14 was the speaking in a foreign language as at Pentecost. See John Calvin's commentary; Donald Burdick, *Tongues: to Speak or Not to Speak* (Moody Press, 1969), pp. 18-22; and S. Lewis Johnson, "The Gift of Tongues and the Book of Acts" *Bibliotheca Sacra* (Oct.-Dec., 1963) p. 311. If this theory is true, then it only shows a greater cleavage between the New Testament and modern glossolalia, which is rarely, if ever, in foreign languages. (On the other hand, two factors lead many to believe that the tongue-speaking of I Corinthians was an ecstatic phenomenon and not the use of a foreign language: 1. By comparing tongue-speaking with musical notes that have no distinction (14:7-8), Paul points to an unintelligible ecstatic speaking because a foreign language has sounds that are very distinctive. 2. Would an unbeliever, hearing someone speaking another language say he is out of his mind [14:23]?)

speaking but plays it down. This should speak volumes to any who today want to speak in tongues. To see the truth of this statement, observe the following:

1. In these chapters Paul speaks of special spiritual gifts and not only of tongue-speaking. Glossolalia is only one of many special gifts listed in this section. One of his major points is that God is pleased with diversity and that just as the hand, ear, or eye cannot exalt itself over other parts of the body, so neither can any who have been blessed with a particular spiritual gift exalt himself over others.

2. The three times Paul lists the gifts, he places tongue-speaking or the concomitant interpretation last (12:8-10; 12:28-30; 14:26).[7] This does not necessarily mean that he consciously considers tongue-speaking to be the least important, but with his whole emphasis on intelligence and wisdom, what he does value highly comes first, such as wisdom and knowledge in one list, being an apostle or prophet in another, or having a hymn, a word of instruction, or a revelation in a third list.

3. The real baptism of the Spirit comes not as a sudden blessing, subsequent to accepting Christ as Savior. It comes at the very time of that acceptance. "For we were all baptized by one Spirit into one body" (12:13). Baptism by the Spirit means being made a Christian by the Holy Spirit.

4. Love is more important than tongues (chap. 13). How remarkable are Paul's words! In all the Bible we have one place alone where it gives instructions about glossolalia, and then at this very place Paul says there is something better. He writes: "Do all speak in tongues? Do all interpret? But eagerly desire the greater gifts. And now I will show you the most excellent way" (12:30-31), namely, love (chap. 13). In other words, after a Christian has been saved, the best that he can seek for is not a sudden inrushing of the Holy Spirit, testified to by the speaking in tongues, but it is love—love that is the fruit of the Spirit (Gal. 5:22). Paul goes on in chapter 14 to commend tongue-speaking, but far better than that is the ordinary virtue of love. Thus right in the middle of this special gifts section (chaps. 12— 14), Paul singles out and highlights love as the finest of all.

___

[7] When Paul lists spiritual gifts in Rom. 12:6-8, it is remarkable that he does not even mention tongue-speaking.

This is what the Christian should concentrate on. This is where his priorities should lie—not in special gifts, but in love.

5. In 14:1 Paul singles out not tongue-speaking but prophecy as the best spiritual gift to seek for. He writes: "Eagerly desire spiritual gifts, especially the gift of prophecy (14: 1). Tongue-speaking is all right, says Paul, and desirable, for a person edifies himself; but he who prophesies edifies the church, and that is better (14:4). So, Paul continues, "I would like every one of you to speak in tongues, but I would rather have you prophesy" (14:5). His lengthy reasoning is that speaking in tongues is unintelligible for others and therefore not edifying. But prophesying (not only telling the future, but speaking for God) can be understood and, therefore, is edifying for the church. So, says Paul, "Try to excel in gifts that build up the church" (14:12), and tongue-speaking is not one of them.

6. Even in this one great passage on spiritual gifts Paul does not command anyone to speak in tongues. He says that a tongue-speaker "edifies himself," and that "I would like everyone of you to speak in tongues, but I would rather have you prophesy" (14:5). He does command the church not to forbid tongue-speaking (14:39), but nowhere does he command tongue-speaking. The closest he comes to a command is in 14:1: "Eagerly desire spiritual gifts." But this pertains to all gifts and not tongues only, and it is not strictly a command for everyone, as is the command "Love your neighbor as yourself." In matters of salvation or sanctification or keeping the law or prayer or baptism or the Lord's Supper or looking for Christ's return, the Bible gives plenty of commands, but never does it command someone to speak in tongues.

7. Paul's guidelines restrict the use of glossolalia. In 14:26-27 he lays down four restrictions:

    a. Speaking in tongues should be for the strengthening of the church.

    b. In a worship service only two—or at the most three—should speak.

    c. It should be done one at a time.

    d. There must be an interpreter.

H. *Romans, Galatians, Ephesians, Philippians, Colossians, I, II Thessalonians, I, II Timothy, Titus, Philemon, Hebrews,*

*James, I, II Peter, I, II, III John, Jude, and Revelation nowhere
even mention tongue-speaking.*

So, to return to our major thesis stated at the start of this
chapter: *There may be genuine speaking in tongues today—*
although many Christians question that. *Yet, if there is, the same
emphasis should be given it that the Bible does.* We should not
neglect what the Bible teaches, nor should we exalt what the
Bible does not.

We find, then, that the four Gospels do not give either an
example of tongue-speaking or instructions for it. Our Lord
Jesus Christ—not even if we accept the genuineness of Mark
16:17—never once commands tongue-speaking. In Acts we have
only three cases of glossolalia and all these are different from
the modern ecstatic speaking. Even if they were of the same
kind, these would only be examples and not necessarily norma-
tive for our lives; that is, examples are not commands.[8] Note
then that outside of I Corinthians 12—14 there is not so much
as a hint of glossolalia. Now if glossolalia were so crucial to our
spiritual welfare, if a second inrushing of the Holy Spirit, signified by speaking in tongues, were so vital to our holy living, then
Jesus Christ and the Bible have failed to get the point across.
For in all the Bible from Genesis through Revelation there is
only one clear passage that deals with tongue-speaking as a
continuing gift (not as an initial gift), and in that one place
Paul deemphasizes it and exalts love as much more important.
In no place in all the Bible is there even one command to speak
in tongues. It is completely silent at this point. So, if there is a
God-given gift of tongues today, well and good. It should be
used. And it should be emphasized to the same extent that

---

[8] We must be careful that we do not elevate history to a position of
commands, saying that we are obliged to emulate that which happens in
history. We must not canonize history. John Stott states it well when he
writes: "The revelation of the purpose of God in scripture should be sought
in its *didactic,* rather than its *historical* parts. More precisely, we should
look for it in the teaching of Jesus, and in the sermons and writings of
the apostles, and not in the purely narrative portions of Acts. What is
described in Scripture as having happened to others is not necessarily intended for us, whereas what is *promised* to us we are to appropriate, and
what is *commanded* we are to obey," *The Baptism and Fulness of the Holy
Spirit* (Inter-Varsity Press, 1965), p. 4. And the *Report of the Special
Committee on the Work of the Holy Spirit* of the United Presbyterian
Church in the United States of America (1970, p. 7) concurs in this.

Matthew, Mark, Luke, John, James, Peter, Paul, the author of Hebrews, and our Lord Jesus Christ did.

In practicing tongues, however, one must be very sensitive to the deception of externalities. For innately we all would like something dramatic and tangible for our faith. We find more comfort in external signs than in the internal working of the Spirit, in the opening of skies than in the opening of the heart. But the Christian life is not one of fire, wind, earthquakes, visions, and angelic appearances; but it is a life of the powerful but quiet working of the Holy Spirit. Christianity is not so much visible tangibles, as it is being patient with a temperamental child, gladly taking out the garbage, and talking to a widow after church. Sanctification consists not so much in the dramatic speaking in tongues as in being kind when someone barks at you, loving instead of hating when a lady jumps in line ahead of you, and refraining from spitefully jamming on the high beam when the oncoming car fails to respond to the dimming of your own lights.

In the past God has allowed a few to have special gifts from the Holy Spirit, but in all ages he commands everyone to be holy. What is needed is not so much the gifts of the Spirit as the fruit of the Spirit (Gal. 5:22). And that will come about only to the extent that Christ and the Spirit dwell in us. Christ is the vine and we are the branches (John 15); the Spirit is the tree, and our good deeds are his fruit (Gal. 5). We must seek not to be "drunk on wine" but to be "filled with the Spirit" (Eph. 5:18). Hereby Paul is not teaching a sudden, richer indwelling of the Spirit subsequent to being saved. Rather, he is speaking of that everyday ongoing work of the Spirit in our lives, whereby we grow in (not jump into) the grace and knowledge of our Lord Jesus Christ. The Christian must not be deluded into thinking that there is a shortcut to holiness, that by three lessons he can arrive at spiritual maturity, or that tongues is a substitute for holiness. Holiness comes not in a sudden glossolalic experience, but by a long, continuous fighting against sin and running the Christian race course.[9]

[9] Donald Burdick says the same in his fine study on *Tongues: to Speak or Not to Speak* (Moody Press, 1969), p. 86: "Spiritual accomplishment is not easy to come by. It is the result of agonizing growth, of defeat after defeat followed by victory, of wrestling in prayer and searching the Word of God. Christian character is forged by blow after blow on the anvil of

That is where the action is: Not in the externalities, but in the inward working of the Spirit; not in the drama of tongues but in the action of love, and this will come about to the extent we are indwelt by the Spirit. When a person experiences Ephesians 5:18, Galatians 5:22 will follow. So we should pray, not so much for tongues as for love, not so much for the gift of the Spirit as for the fruit of the Spirit, not so much for visible proofs as for the calm, effective working of the Holy Spirit. "This is to my Father's glory, that you bear much fruit" (John 15:8).

> Spirit of God, dwell Thou within my heart;
>   Wean it from earth, through all its pulses move;
> Stoop to my weakness, mighty as Thou art,
>   And make me love Thee as I ought to love.
>
> I ask no dream, no prophet ecstasies,
>   No sudden rending of the veil of clay,
> No angel visitant, no opening skies;
>   But take the dimness of my soul away.
>
> Teach me to love Thee as Thine angels love,
>   One holy passion filling all my frame—
> The baptism of the heaven-descended Dove,
>   My heart an altar, and Thy love the flame.

daily experience. It never comes quickly, but, like maturity of any kind, it is the product of the slow process of growth."

The Holy Spirit and Guidance 10

People are seeking guidance today. The world in all of its complexities presents to them many opportunities and choices. They are asking: Should I marry this girl or not? Should I go to college or go into business? How much money should I give to the church? Which job should I take? They want to know what is right. But they do not know how to make up their minds. Desiring to be led, they seek guidance. They want someone else to help them make up their minds and to show them which way to go. They sometimes say: I would be willing to do what is right, if I only knew what that was.

Christianity offers the answer to this deep-seated need. It offers guidance to those who are perplexed in the choices that confront them. Strictly speaking, the term *guidance* must be understood to mean two radically different matters. One is Biblical guidance, that is, the directions and instructions which God gives us in the Bible for all moral decisions. With this type of guidance the Holy Spirit is very directly connected. The other is providential guidance, that is, God's controlling of all of life's forces so that the individual is necessarily caused to go in a certain course. The first type of guidance concerns God's preceptive will (what

115

we ought to do); the second concerns his decretive will (what God certainly brings to pass).

I. Biblical Guidance

A. *In Moral Decisions*

The Holy Spirit is the author of guidance in the first sense, that is, in indicating to the Christian God's will for his life. Jesus said: "But when he, the Spirit of truth, comes, he will guide you into all truth" (John 16:13); and, "the Counselor, the Holy Spirit, whom the Father will send in my name, will teach you all things and will remind you of everything I have said to you" (John 14:26). Paul wrote: "Those who are led by the Spirit of God are sons of God" (Rom. 8:14). There is no doubt that Scripture teaches that the Spirit guides the children of God.

In chapter 4 we considered the Holy Spirit's wondrous gift of revelation to the world. We saw that, according to the Bible's own testimony to itself, it is infallible in the original languages. It is not only the word of man, but it is also the Word of God, the inscripturated voice of God. This means, of course, that by this Word of the Spirit we can know with absolute certainty which course we should follow in many instances. The Word is replete with instructions to us, indicating definitely and un-ambiguously what to do in many and varied circumstances. "All Scripture . . . is useful for teaching, rebuking, correcting and training in righteousness, so that the man of God may be thoroughly equipped for every good work" (II Tim. 3:16, 17).

A young girl, for example, may be deeply in love with a boy who is not a Christian, and she wants to know whether or not she ought to marry him. By going to the Bible, she can be guided as to what is right. For I Corinthians 7:39 says that a girl may marry anyone she wishes, "but he must belong to the Lord." To do otherwise is sin. In this way the Spirit guides us through the Word.

Or perhaps someone is confronted with the choice of joining one of two churches. One has a beautiful building, an entertaining service, and the members are people of social distinction, but it denies the true gospel of Christ. The other is small and looked down on by the community, but it preaches uncompromisingly the whole counsel of God. In this case, too, the Word of the Spirit gives clear-cut guidance as to which one should be joined.

Or perchance a soldier on guard duty in a warehouse has the opportunity of obtaining a trim, new jacket without anyone knowing it. Other soldiers do it. Should he do the same, or should he not? The Word comes and guides him very clearly in this matter, too, for the eighth commandment is "Do not steal."

From these examples we see that through the Word of God the Spirit guides us in moral problems that confront us. We have mentioned only three. But the Bible, of course, is filled on every page with guidance. It leads us by commandments such as the Decalogue, by instructions of the apostles to the churches, by the example of Christ himself, by the examples of godly saints in the Old and New Testaments, by the warning of ungodly examples, and in many other ways. Thus, in one manner or another, the Holy Spirit through the Bible actually does give clear-cut guidance for many of the situations in which we find ourselves, and about which we may think that the Word of God says nothing.

This means that we must know that Word thoroughly if we are to find the Spirit's guidance. It is not sufficient simply to know the Ten Commandments. We must know the Bible through and through, in its breadth and depth. If we do not, we have no right to expect a special, extraordinary guidance to fill in for our laziness. The Holy Spirit does not do for us apart from the Word what he has already done for us through the Word, the infallible guide for our lives. If many times we think that the Bible gives no guidance to our problem, it is often simply because we do not know the Word of God well enough. Therefore, we must be diligent in studying that guide so that we will know how to decide when life's choices are before us.

We saw also in chapter 5 that for a person who wants to know matters with certainty, it is not sufficient for him to have a book, however true and plain that book may be. If a person is blind, he cannot read it, and hence, a second element necessary for receiving help from that book is eyesight. We noted then that the Holy Spirit not only provides an infallible Word, but also by regeneration gives to a spiritually blind person the spiritual eyesight necessary to read aright what is there before him. Man needs the illumination of the Holy Spirit in order to read.

This explains why in the matter of Biblical guidance he needs illumination by the Spirit, too. Even though the Bible is filled with guidance for our lives, many who read it never see that guidance because they are blind. This is true not only for the non-Christian, who does not have the Spirit in his life at all, but to some extent also for the Christian. Sin is the cause of spiritual blindness. And since in a Christian there is still a residue of sin, he is also partially blind. To remove this blindness, it is necessary that the Holy Spirit operate on the soul. He must illuminate the darkened mind, causing the reader of the Bible to grasp the meaning of certain guiding principles as they are read, and making him aware of the relevancy of the Scriptural principles to the choices that are before him. And he must also sanctify the Christian's will so that he will not be prejudiced against a right choice by his sinful desires.

When the Christian reads the Spirit's Guidebook with a mind and heart that are increasingly illumined and sanctified by the Spirit, he will have a means by which he may know how to make correct decisions. As a matter of fact, this is the only means of guidance that the Spirit gives the Christian in choices between good and evil: there is no other.

From the three examples we have already cited, it is obvious that the Bible is a lucid guide in the many cases where it clearly prescribes the morally good choice between two acts. There are, however, many other cases in which the guidance is not so clear. For example, the Bible tells me to give sacrificially. But how much is sacrificially for me? How can I know exactly how much *I* should give to the church each year? The answer varies greatly with each individual, depending upon such factors as the size of the income, the size of the family, and the amount of sickness in the family.

Admittedly, this is a most difficult decision, especially since we are not completely sanctified and the great pull of the material things of this world prejudices a clear, objective decision. Yet here, too, we may find the guidance of the Spirit through the Bible and not apart from it. As we sincerely seek the Spirit's guidance in the matter of giving, as we study fully the circumstances around the material giving of the Biblical saints, and as we meditate on Paul's abundant instruction in II Corinthians 8 and 9, the Spirit may well make us aware of the relevancy of a particular example or command to our specific need. At the same time, he may be delivering us from intensely greedy desires so that we will be ready to concur with the Biblical guidance as the Spirit brings it to bear on our minds.

Thus, the Bible is a sufficient guide for every moral decision of our lives. In some cases the guidance is explicit. In other cases it must be deduced by good and necessary consequence from Scripture. But it is sufficient in pointing out the morality of all choices.

B. In the Adiaphora

However, there are times when there is not a choice between right and wrong, but between two morally good alternatives. These are called the adiaphora. A young man may be confronted with the opportunity of being a foreman at Ford or at General Motors. Or there may be the question of whether to vacation in Vermont or in Florida, to marry a Christian from Wellesley or Radcliffe, to be a church elder or Sunday school superintendent, to be a missionary in Nigeria or in Japan, or to sail for India in June or in September. In these cases, *other things being equal,* there may be no right or wrong involved. If so, the Bible allows both choices, for both are good. Then we must not seek for a new revelation apart from the Spirit-given Bible to guide us in these choices.

Naturally, however, the choice between these two moral goods may have a great influence on one's life. There may be all the difference in the world if the person goes to Ford instead of General Motors, marries the Wellesley instead of the Radcliffe graduate, or serves in Nigeria instead of Japan. Therefore, we certainly want to be led by God into that path that will be the most conducive to the good of all persons concerned and will cause us to glorify him the most. But this does not mean that we should ask God to indicate to us in some supernatural way the choice we should take.

For to ask for a new revelation, a new guide, would be to deny the all-sufficiency of the Spirit-breathed Bible. Then we tread in the dangerous error of Rome, which instead of relying only on the Bible and the illumination of the Holy Spirit asks for the additional revelation of the church tradition; and we incur the danger of the mystics who, not being satisfied with the Spirit's revelation in the Scriptures, seek for a new, individual revelation. Rather, we believe that the Westminster theologians were fully correct when they eloquently and carefully stated that "the *whole counsel* of God concerning all things necessary for his glory, man's salvation, faith and *life,* is either expressly set down in Scripture, or by good and necessary consequence may be deduced from Scripture, *unto which nothing at any time may be added, whether by new revelations of the Spirit, or traditions of men" (Westminster Confession of Faith* I, **IV**).

There are, however, three things we should do in attempting to choose between two morally good alternatives. First, we must engage all our faculties in studying all the factors surrounding the two or more choices. Secondly, as we do this, we should pray that the Holy Spirit will strengthen our natural powers of reason, judgment, and common sense so that we will make a wise decision. Finally, we should ask God so to control all the circumstances of life so that, even though we may not know with certainty whether we are doing the best or not, we will as a matter of fact be moving in the best direction. In other words, we may pray that God will so govern all of life that "all things [will] work together for good to them that love God, to them who are the called according to his purpose" (Rom. 8:28, KJV).

II. Errors to Avoid

History reveals that three errors have arisen in connection with the Spirit's guidance. Each one stems from a failure to observe the Biblical principle that the Spirit guides the Christian infallibly only through his Guidebook, the Bible; and each one, when followed through, impinges upon the authority of the Spirit. Two of these errors deal with the second type of guidance mentioned earlier, namely, providential guidance, and the third deals with special, extra-Biblical revelations by the Spirit.

Although Biblical guidance is the one and only means by which a Christian may know the will of God in the moral decisions of his life, yet there is this second type of guidance—providential— which is similar to Biblical guidance in name only. Nevertheless, if carefully understood, it may also truly be called guidance.

It is a fact that the omnipotent Creator controls all things in the world. Not only does he ordain the great events of history, the rise and fall of nations, great wars, the achievements of science and medicine (which are revolutionizing our lives), and the election of presidents; but he also ordains the small things that seem insignificant to us, such as the falling of a sparrow to the ground, the movement of a blade of grass by a summer wind, and the exact course of a raindrop on a window pane in a spring shower. Having this power, God can and does guide the lives of people down to the smallest details. If carefully distinguished, this control by God may be called "providential guidance," although its indiscriminate use can lead to confusion.

What a happy fact it is that we have providential guidance! A good and loving God governs our lives and leads us into those ways that are good for us. He was guiding, for example, all the circumstances surrounding the selling of Joseph into Egypt, even to the details of the speed and direction of Jacob's wandering sheep, so that at exactly the right time they would be in the pathway of a certain band of Ishmaelites going to Egypt. He controlled the Ishmaelites' desire to go from Gilead to Egypt on a certain day, or a certain hour, no sooner and no later. Had these and other details been different, Joseph would never have been sold into Egypt, and the whole course of redemption, which was conditioned by the sojourn of the Israelites in Egypt, would have been changed. Yes, God guides by his providence in even the smallest details.

He controls the running schedules of trains, so that a boy meets his life partner at a certain station. He determines a mother's need and desire for a box of soap powder so that she goes to a certain store at a precise time. While she is on the way she testifies to a stranger, and this witnessing proves to be the initial means by which he is eventually saved. By his providence, God causes a Latin teacher to become partially deaf, so that he is forced to give up his profession and go to another city to learn a new trade. In that city someone takes him to a church where he later finds Christ. This changes his whole life and means the eventual entry into the gospel ministry of his son, who, in turn, is able to influence many lives. All of this happens because of the deafness which God purposely caused. Now this is God's leading, and we may rejoice that God so graciously does lead us, often into places where we do not want to go, yet which later appear to be good. He opens up ways for us that we could never have dreamed of. Yes, God guides by his providence.

But now we must make a careful distinction. Although it is unquestionably true that God guides us by his providence, we may *never*—and we underscore that word *never*—say that the course of events shows us infallibly what God either wants us to do in the future or wanted us to do in the past. Providence tells us how he has already, in actuality, guided or ruled us in the past. It tells us what he has done. But it is not a way of knowing incontrovertibly what we should do in the future or what we should have done in the past. To assert the latter is not Biblical, and it is thoroughly dangerous. It is the equivalent of saying that apart from and next to the Bible, God gives us another revelation. Such an assertion fails to give full due to the guiding work of the Holy Spirit in his Word. Let us illustrate how this providential guidance can be misused in two ways.

A. In the first place, some well-meaning Christians assert that they can determine beyond a shadow of doubt what God wants them to do in the future by correctly observing providential happenings. For example, one prominent American minister did not know on a rainy Saturday morning whether or not to cancel a church picnic planned for the afternoon. So he put God to a test, he says. He told God that if he saw any blue sky before noon, he would go ahead with the plans. If not, he would cancel them. In this case he saw an opening in the ominous clouds, went ahead with the plans, and enjoyed a sunny picnic. Later he related this event to his congregation, drawing as his conclusion that by providential signs God shows us what to do.

Another servant of God, a missionary, once related that in order to know whether or not it was God's will for him to marry a certain girl, he looked to God for a sign. If God's answer was to be yes, he decided, then God had to show him his will by causing at least one boy to be led to Christ through his preaching at a certain school on a certain day. God did so, and so he married the girl. Later on this same person even had the audacity to test God in a similar fashion *after* they were married, asking the Lord to set a seal on their union. (As if it would have been justifiable for him to go contrary to God's revealed will in the Bible and obtain a separation if he had not received that seal from the Lord!)

One girl, who was puzzled whether or not to go to India as a missionary, said she would never go unless she saw the word *India* written in letters six feet high. Soon thereafter, as she entered a camp that was sponsoring a missionary rally, she saw the word *India* written out in big letters six feet high, greeting everyone who entered the conference. She then knew, she said, what God's will was.

Others open the Bible at random, blindly point to a verse, and on the basis of the chance word or phrase claim that God has indicated his will for them.

Still others reason that, since God makes certain paths very difficult, placing one obstacle after another in the way, he is "closing" that door for their lives. Or perhaps God makes another way easy. In that case, they say, he is "opening" that door for them, and they can see how God is "showing" them what to do. They now know his will for them beyond all question, they assert, and are at rest in their minds.

For example, a man wanted to buy a certain house, but he was not sure if it was the Lord's will. He decided to put forth a reasonable (not his utmost) effort to purchase the house. He had only $500 in cash, so he went to a banker and candidly explained his situation in order to borrow the necessary money. Before he went he had made up his mind that if, after explaining the situation, the banker loaned him the money, it was God's will that he should buy. If the banker did not, he would not use any other means to buy that house. He was not granted the loan, so he went to another locality. God had pointed the way, he thought.

Such ways to determine God's will for our conduct are not Biblical and, moreover, are subject to an irrational arbitrariness. There is no Biblical evidence that God gives us signs to indicate the course of action we should take. At times a certain providential event may seem to be a pointer, but it must be remembered that God often purposely places obstacles in our way for his own reasons. Sometimes he does so, not to tell us not to go in a certain direction, but to chastise us, and thereby draw us closer to him. At other times he puts obstacle after obstacle in our way to make us stronger and to test our perseverance. Imagine what the woman in the parable of the unrighteous judge (Luke 18) would have done, if she had followed these unbiblical theories of guidance! Instead of persisting in her request that the judge hear her case, she would have reasoned that because of her many failures God did not want her to receive her desire, and therefore, she would have desisted from going to the judge. But the very point of the parable was that the woman was wise in persisting, and that we should do the same.

Or where would be the work of the great missionary to India, William Carey, if he had bowed before "closed doors"? Consider the obstacles in his pathway to ministering in India. The East India Company, which controlled India, was antagonistic to missionary efforts; his wife adamantly refused to go and only changed her mind a few days before the sailing date; later she became depressed, gave her husband no sympathy, and finally became mentally ill; dysentery struck the whole family; and Carey had to borrow money in order to avoid starvation. Many would have considered these obstacles a definite leading by God not to go to or continue in India. Yet Carey persevered, "expecting great things from God and attempting great things for God, and God blessed his work signally.

Perhaps a young man wonders whether God is calling him to be a preacher. Because of a speech defect he may reason that God is closing the door to the parish ministry and is thereby indicating that he should enter another field of labor. This *may* be God's desire, but it could also be that God wants him to be a second Demosthenes—who by hard discipline overcame his speech difficulties—and to enter the ministry after all.

Thus it is possible, through this extra-Biblical method of seeking guidance from providence, for people to deceive themselves into thinking that a certain door is closed, whereas in reality God is testing their purpose and perseverance and is leading them to better things by chastisement. Therefore, we must be exceptionally cautious in attempting to discern God's will for us in the *future* by looking at events.

B. Neither—and this is a second misuse of providential guidance—may we, on the basis of providential events, make categorical statements as to what God wanted us to do in the *past*. This is frequently done.

In 1638 Mrs. Anne Hutchinson was banished from Massachusetts for religious reasons. When, five years later, the Indians murdered her, many regarded that as divine proof that they had been correct in banishing her.

Sometimes, when events do not turn out as people had hoped, the remark is made: "Well, what we wanted was not supposed to be," or, "It was not meant to be that way." The implication is that they had hoped for the wrong thing.

In many cases, well-intentioned Christians seize upon events that have turned out according to their wishes and assert with great positiveness that such happenings are an evidence of the favor of God upon them and their choices. This is dangerous reasoning. Man can see such a short distance that it could be that these so-called providential "blessings" are not a blessing at all, but a curse. Yet it could also be that these events are truly an evidence of God's magnificent blessings. The point is this: We do not know absolutely. God has not told us. It is impossible to determine infallibly God's sanction or disapproval of our deeds on the basis of past events.

In a very enlightening discussion of the problem, Berkouwer points out that all events—the smallest and the largest—are in God's providence, in the hand of God.[1] To select one fragment of that providence, he says, whether it be of a seemingly important or critical nature or not, for an indication of God's leading for us would amount to a "fragmentization of history" and a "canonization" of a portion of God's providence, that is, elevating a fragment of providence to the level of Scripture. This would be an unlawful distinction between the hand of God in all providence and the directional finger of God in a fragment of providence. Unless the Bible points out the meaning of history, it would be arbitrary and subjective to isolate one portion of all of God's handlings and on that basis indicate we know God's guidance. The mingling of the blood of the Galileans with sacrifices, or the dramatic falling of the tower of Siloam on eighteen men (Luke 13), or the birth of a blind boy (John 9) might seem to be indicative of the displeasure of God; yet Jesus warns us that such an easy interpretation is not a correct analysis of these events. When God's Word interprets history, as in the case of Herod's death (Acts 12) or in the bringing of enemies against Israel to punish her (Habakkuk) or in the signs of the times, then and then only do we have an infallible interpretation of these events. But apart from this, we mortals, who are still partially blinded by sin, can only make an arbitrary and subjective selection of certain fragments of all God's providence and therefore will interpret inaccurately.

The mariners with whom Jonah was sailing happened to have reasoned correctly when they judged that the storm that was battering their ship was due to God's anger against Jonah. But the

[1] Berkouwer, G. C., *The Providence of God* (Eerdmans, 1952), chapter 6.

Maltan barbarians interpreted a similar disaster incorrectly when they thought that Paul's shipwreck and the seemingly confirming sign of the bite from the poisonous snake meant that Paul was a murderer (Acts 28). One will interpret the fall of Rome as sure evidence of the immorality of *paganism* (Augustine). Others will interpret the same event as a clear indication that the *Christians* had sinned (Salvianus of the fifth century). Others will select striking and apparently favorable events as a sign that they did what God wanted them to do, but they will quickly pass over the events that are less striking and are seemingly unfavorable to them, asserting that these events are of little if any significance in interpreting God's will for their lives. To select one event and not another in this fashion without a Biblical directive is an arbitrary, subjective decision without any objective norm to tell what a certain providential happening means. For adversity is sometimes a sign of God's love (Heb. 12:5-13) and not of a closing door, and what is seemingly favorable now may well be detrimental to the Christian's welfare in five or fifty years. God causes *all* things—adversity as well as prosperity—to work together for the good of the Christian. Therefore, in the absence of the infallible interpretation of providence by God's Word, we must be cautious in choosing one fragment of God's providence as indicative of the mind of God to the neglect of others.

We do not mean that God does not guide (in the sense of rule) his people by providential circumstances. He most certainly does. Nor do we mean that providential events are not to be taken into consideration in our decisions. We must use our minds and common sense in analyzing all the factors in a situation in order that we may make a wise choice. But it is not possible for us to point to certain providential events and say that these conclusively show us what course of action we should take or should have taken. That would be asserting a new revelation—a revelation outside of the Bible—by which the Spirit has guided us. And today God does not give us extra-Biblical revelations. The Spirit uses only the Bible to guide us inerrantly. In other words, we do not deny providential guidance (control), but we do deny the possibility of an infallible knowledge through providential circumstances of what God wanted us to do in the past or wants us to do in the future.

C. So far we have mentioned only the error of seeking infallible guidance by providence. But there is another equally popular and equally fallacious practice. Some seek God's guidance not only by circumstances, but also by special revelations from the Spirit. Having studied the Word of God, they sometimes sit still and "listen." They wait for God to speak to them in the quiet hour. "Speak, Lord, for thy servant is listening" is their motto. Some apparently believe that the Spirit actually whispers in their ear. Others, however, offended by such crassness, believe that the Spirit speaks to them by hunches or impulses or mental impressions. Then they "know" God's will for them for that day. They have received their "marching orders." Perhaps, they believe, the Spirit told them how to do their business or to whom to speak or what letter to write. Sometimes they speak with dead certainty of the "Lord's leading": "The Lord wanted me to speak to you today," or, "The Lord is leading me to this Bible conference." Coupled with the guidance by providence, these impressions, they feel, can reveal to them God's will for all situations. In fact, F. B. Meyer says that "the circumstances of our daily life are to us an infallible [N.B.] indication of God's will, when they concur with the inward promptings of the Spirit and the Word of God" *(The Secret of Guidance).*

At times an appeal is made to the special, divine leading that is found in both the Old and New Testaments, such as the extraordinary guidance that God gave to Gideon by means of the fleece; the clear-cut directives that the Spirit gave to Philip in telling him to speak to the Ethiopian eunuch; and the Spirit's refusal to let Paul go into Bythinia.

It is open to question, however, whether we are to expect this sort of guidance today. At certain periods of Biblical history God did reveal his will by special revelations, just as he performed miracles in certain eras. But we no longer live in those days of inspiration, revelations, and miracles. The canon of Scripture is closed, and apart from the Bible we may not speak of "an *infallible* indication of God's will," as Meyer has so candidly put it. We must exercise extreme caution in stating so quickly and positively that we *know* that "the Lord led us" to this or that action. It is possible that God so controls providential circumstances and that the Spirit so creates in us certain feelings, impressions, urges, and impulses that we feel impelled to move in a certain direction. But these phenomena are too often misused, so that a person claims in effect that he has a special directive from the Spirit and is positive of his will for him. Such assertions dishonor the Spirit's only infallible rule for our lives, his Word. As we saw in a previous chapter, the illumination which the Holy Spirit gives to us is one of enlightenment, but not of additional revelation. He does not teach new truths, but he uses the old truths of the Bible. Taking these, he sharpens man's perceptive faculties, so that he can see and understand the old better.

Not only is it unscriptural to seek for "signs" and special revelations in order that we may make up our minds, but such "guidance," if it may be called that, instead of leading may mislead. Sometimes we use this theory of guidance to carry out our own desires under the pretense of holiness. This is not always done with the intention to deceive, but it may be done subconsciously. Even we Christians, who have not been freed from sin entirely, are very adept at rationalizing our actions. Hence our impressions and divine "hunches" often turn out to be nothing else than a strong desire to do what we want to do. For instance, when a person says that he "feels led of the Lord" to get married, his feeling may be nothing more than a strong personal desire to get married. Moreover, these so-called divine impressions, instead of being the work of God, may sometimes be the work of the devil, who makes capital of our psychological instability. Furthermore, by seeking these signs, it is possible for a Christian to avoid a clear-cut call to duty. For example, God may convict a person that he should go to the mission field, and yet the person refuses to go unless God reassures him by giving a special sign such as the name of the mission field in letters six feet high. In these ways such "signs" and special "revelations" may be misleading and even detrimental.

Many Christians dislike to make up their minds in the many decisions that confront them. Desiring an easy way to ascertain the will of God, they too often resort to seeking God's guidance through illegitimate ways. However, we still believe that the Westminster theologians gave sane, safe, and Biblical advice when they stated that we may not add any revelations to the Bible, and that the whole counsel of God concerning all things necessary for life is either expressly set down in Scripture, or by good and necessary consequence may be deduced from it.

Conclusion

In conclusion, there are three rules that we should follow as we attempt to make life's decisions. First we must be *thoroughly* acquainted with the Spirit's only Guidebook, the Bible. It is replete with instruction for our lives. It is a sufficient guide for every moral choice, telling us explicitly or by good and necessary deductions which course of action is morally good or evil. If we do not know that Word well, we shall certainly be needlessly perplexed as to our duty in many instances. But the greater our familiarity with the *whole* Bible, the clearer will be our guidance.

Secondly, since we are blinded by sin, we must continually pray that we may be increasingly illumined and sanctified by the Holy Spirit. He will then sharpen our insights into the principles he has set forth in the Scriptures, he will enable us to apply them correctly to our concrete situations, and he will deliver us from evil desires which becloud a proper decision. If we follow these first two rules, we will find that we have all the guidance necessary to make the proper decision whenever a choice between good and evil confronts us.

But in those cases where we are confronted with two or more morally good alternatives, about which the Bible gives little guidance except to point out that they are both morally good, we must not look to providence for an infallible pointer, nor to a special communication by the Holy Spirit for an indication of which choice is best for us. But, and this is the third rule, we should to the utmost of our ability use all the faculties with which God has endowed us. We must search out the problem, gather all the information possible, talk to those who understand, and use our minds. Regeneration does not destroy our intellects, and God expects us to use what he has given us. There is no quick, easy way. There are no ready-made, pat answers. There is no book or person to tell us what to do in a given situation. To be guided in these cases requires work.

If, for example, we want to know whether or not to go on a Saturday afternoon picnic, we must not "test" God, but rather use the latest meteorological studies. If we want to know whether God has called us to India or not, we must not depend upon such arbitrary circumstances as the erection of six-feet-tall letters, but we must study India's needs, the open door, and our qualifications. If any young man wants to know if it is wise for him to marry a certain girl, he should not suppose that he can dictate to the Holy Spirit in matters of regenerating people, but he should consider all the factors involved, with the reasoning power given to him by God for such a time as this, in addition to following his personal inclination. If a church wants to know which piece of property to buy for a new church building, it should not ask God for a special revelation, but should analyze such factors as the nature of the church and community, the cost of the properties, and the evangelistic potentials.

At the same time, we should pray fervently and continuously to God that in his multitude of ways he will control all the circumstances of life—the momentous ones and the seemingly insignificant ones—and that he will grant the Holy Spirit to sharpen our reasoning powers so that we will choose those paths that will be best for the kingdom and ourselves. If we are God's children and do not grieve him, we will find that time and again he will enable us to make the best choice, even if we are sometimes not aware that it is the best.

This does not mean that in these matters God will guide in the sense that he will indicate a duty for us by means of an incontrovertible sign in providential happenings. Not at all. But it does mean that he will influence all of the circumstances surrounding our lives so that we will make wise decisions. The minister, for example, may never say with infallibility that he knows that he was guided by God to stay in his present charge, rather than to go to Boston or Los Angeles. He is not infallible. He is human, sinful, and subject to error. He has no special revelation nor providential indications that can tell him beyond a shadow of a doubt that he was right in his decision. But he can feel reasonably sure that, if he is not living in sin, if he used all of his powers to come to a correct decision, and if he and the congregation prayed earnestly and sincerely for guidance, the Holy Spirit directed him to make a wise decision.

Thus, there is no easy, infallible way of finding out God's will for our lives. There is no cut and dried answer. But it is comforting to know that when we follow these three rules—when we read the Spirit's Guidebook thoroughly, pray, and use all our abilities to the utmost—we will find that God will give us guidance in all of life's problems. The Spirit will guide us by his Word and illumination to know how to choose between good and evil; and although in the choice between two goods there will not be a sign telling us what we should do, we may implore God to rule our lives in such a way that we will make those decisions which are the most profitable for his kingdom and us. And God will guide us in this sense.

May we then be grateful to the Father for his providential, ruling guidance, and may we not misuse it. To the Spirit may we be thankful for his active role in revealing to us the will of God's command, illuminating our minds, and making us desire to follow his leading. Let us honor him by increasingly seeking and following his guidance.

The Holy Spirit and Divine Sonship 11

The Bible uses the term *son of God* in at least three different ways. It applies this title to Jesus Christ, to man in general, and to the Christian. In each of these sonships, the Holy Spirit plays an important role. What that role is in each case and why it is significant for us will be the object of our study in this chapter.

I. Christ's Sonship

With reference to Jesus Christ alone, there are also four different ways in which the Bible uses the title *Son of God.*[1]

A. Trinitarian Sonship

When we think of Jesus as the Son of God, we think first of all of his divinity—that he is the eternal Son of the first Person of the Trinity. This is the Sonship that is purely within the Trinity and which has respect to his Godhead only. The Holy Spirit has nothing to do with this Sonship, except that he proceeds from the Son as well as from the Father, as we saw in chapter 1.

---

[1] For an enlightening discussion of these distinctions as they pertain to Jesus, see G. Vos, *The Self-Disclosure of Jesus,* New York, 1926.

B. Messianic Sonship

The title *Son of God,* however, is applied to Jesus in three other ways, and in these the Holy Spirit does have a definite work. Jesus is called the Son of God not simply because of his eternal, intratrinitarian relationship to the Father—because of his divine nature—but also because of his Messianic office. He was the Father's representative on earth, being subordinate to him in his Messianic work. He was sent by the Father to do his will and to fulfill a special mission. Not from eternity had he been the Messiah. Rather, he received something that he had not always had. The Father gave to him a kingdom on earth with a work to perform in it. By virtue of this Messianic relationship to the Father, he is called the Son of God. He told his disciples at the Last Supper, for example, that he conferred a kingdom on them "just as my Father conferred one on me" (Luke 22:29). And when Gabriel announced to Mary that Jesus would be the "Son of the Most High," he explained this title by adding that "the Lord God will give him the throne of his father David; and he will reign over the house of Jacob forever" (Luke 1:33). Thus, in virtue of this Messianic office to which he was appointed in the fullness of time by the Father, Jesus is called the Son of God.

For this Messianic Sonship Jesus had to be especially equipped. More was necessary than simply to have a divine nature; his human nature had to be assisted by the Holy Spirit. In his official capacity as Messiah he needed and depended on the official anointing of the Spirit. And this he received at his baptism, when the Holy Spirit descended upon him in the form of a dove, and the Father, referring to the Messianic Sonship, spoke from heaven, saying: "This is my Son, whom I love; with him I am well-pleased" (Matt. 3:17). As we saw more fully in chapter 6, it was this endowment of the Holy Spirit that equipped Jesus for his public ministry, to preach and to perform miracles. Jesus did not enter into his Messianic ministry simply on the strength of his divine nature, but he relied on the anointing of the Holy Spirit. In this sense, then, the Holy Spirit was essential for Jesus to be the Messianic Son of God.

C. Nativistic Sonship

Jesus is also called the Son of God because in his supernatural birth God was the Father of his human nature. This is intimated when Gabriel tells Mary that "the Holy Spirit will come upon you, and the power of the Most High will overshadow you. So the holy one to be born will be called the Son of God" (Luke 1:35). There is a direct relationship between Mary's being over-shadowed by the Holy Spirit and Jesus' being called the Son of God. Because of the overshadowing, because of the supernatural act of conception by the Holy Spirit, Jesus was called the Son of God. In this nativistic sense, therefore, Jesus can be called the Son of God only because of the activity of the Holy Spirit.

D. *Ethical Sonship*

There is still another way in which Jesus as the Son of God relies upon the Holy Spirit. He is the Son of God in a purely religious and moral sense, very similar to that of the Christian's sonship. If we remember that Jesus had not only a divine but also a human nature, that he was not only omnipotent God but also true man, this religious Sonship of Jesus will be clearer. For as a true human, Jesus worshiped the father and fellowshiped with him. As a religious Son of God, he instructed Peter to pay the temple tax of a half shekel for both himself and Peter, even though "the sons are exempt" (Matt. 17:26). By placing himself upon the same level as Peter, both in the fulfillment of this ceremonial law and in the calling of both Peter and himself "sons," he showed that he was a Son of God in the same sense as Peter. As a Son in this ethical, religious way, he lived inwardly and outwardly in a right relationship to the Father. He obeyed the ceremonial and moral law, he served his Father, he prayed to him, he loved him, and he fellowshiped with him. From his early boyhood to his last breath on the cross when he cried, "My Father, into your hands I commit my spirit," he lived in this Son-Father relationship as far as his human nature was concerned. In this ethical, religious sense, in distinction from his intratrinitarian, Messianic, and nativistic Sonships, he was the Son of God. This he was in a fashion similar to the way in which Christians are sons of God, except, of course, that Christians are adopted sons, and he was a natural one.

In this ethical, religious Sonship, Jesus depended upon the Holy Spirit, too. As we saw in a previous chapter, the grace of

God was upon him (Luke 2:40) in the form of the Holy Spirit, "the Spirit of wisdom and understanding, the Spirit of counsel and might, the Spirit of knowledge and the fear of the LORD" (Isa. 11:2). As Son of God in his human nature, Jesus relied upon the indwelling Holy Spirit to keep him from sin, to give him victory over his temptations, and to enable him to do good.

Thus we see how the Holy Spirit is indispensable for three different Sonships of Jesus Christ. If it had not been for the Holy Spirit, Jesus would not have been equipped for his Messianic Sonship and work. Nor would he have been supernaturally born. Nor would he in his human nature have lived the life of perfection he did and thereby be the sinless Savior whose human life of holiness could be counted as ours. Because of the work of the Holy Spirit in three of the four Sonships of Jesus Christ, we have a perfect Savior who made a perfect substitutionary atonement. Praise the Holy Spirit for Christ as the Son of God!

II. Creative Sonship

A second type of sonship of God that the Bible mentions is what might be called creative sonship, that is, a sonship due to creation. It does not apply to the unique Sonship of Christ, nor to the sonship by grace of the Christian, but to the sonship of all men. All men, regenerated or not, are called sons of God because God created them and because they are like God. As Genesis 1 tells us, man is created in the image of God, that is, he is like God in that he is a spiritual being with a mind, will, and emotions. Thus Paul in his Areopagus address approvingly quotes the pagan Aratus as saying, "We are his children" (Acts 17:28). From the context it is obvious that he means that all men are the sons of God because they are created by God and are like him in that they are spiritual beings. In Hebrews 12:9 the author calls God "the Father of our spirits." This does not refer to God's Fatherhood of believers alone, but to his Fatherhood of all who have life and a spirit, even those who are not Christians.

For this sonship, too, the Holy Spirit is necessary. For, as we have seen, it is the Holy Spirit who is specifically responsible for the creation of man's soul. It is the third Person of the Trinity, and not the Father nor the Son, who endows all men with a spiritual nature, so that they have life, artistic ability, aesthetic appreciation, and intellectual gifts. If man rises to the dramatic heights of a Shakespeare, the philosophical thoughts of an Aristotle, the artistic accomplishments of a Rubens, the musical genius of a Brahms, the statesmanship of a Churchill, or to the simple love of a mother for her child, the ability of a boy to study mathematics, or the skill of a girl in making a dress, then we must praise the Holy Spirit. For these are evidences of the second type of sonship and the Holy Spirit's work in establishing it.

III. The Christian's Sonship

Sonship implies at least two things. First of all, there must be a certain resemblance between the son and the father. It is obvious that the simple fact that an object is created by someone does not mean that it is a son of that person. A car is not the son of an auto manufacturer, but the product of him, because there is no basic likeness between the two. For the same reason a table is not born of a furniture maker, but is produced by him.

On the other hand, a colt, being the true son of a horse, has the features and characteristics of a horse and not of a train or a lion. Like begets like. A human father begets a son who is human like him. Like the father, the son also has a soul and bodily features such as two ears, ten toes, lungs, and a heart. Thus sonship implies likeness between the father and the son.

Secondly, sonship implies that a son has certain filial rights. He is entitled to a name, for example, and to rights of inheritance.

Both of these ideas of sonship are implied in the Biblical term *son of God,* as it is applied to Christians. Sometimes the Bible calls the believer a son of God because he shows a certain resemblance to God. At other times it calls him a son of God because he has certain rights that the natural son of God, Jesus Christ, has. Let us look, then, first of all, at the Christian's sonship in the first sense and see the role of the Holy Spirit in it. This may be called regenerative sonship. Then, let us observe the Christian's sonship in the second sense, and notice the relation of the Holy Spirit there. This is called adoptive sonship. Both apply to Christians, the sons of God.

A. Regenerative Sonship

According to the Bible the Christian is like God. We have
seen that this is so in the creative sense, so that the Christian,
along with natural man, may be called a son of God because he
resembles God, being spiritual, rational, moral, and emotional.
This moral agency of man is called the natural image of God.
It is one way in which all men, in distinction from animals, are
like God.

But the Christian is also similar to God, and therefore a son of
God, in another sense. He is made like God in true knowledge,
righteousness, and holiness (Col. 3:10; Eph. 3:24). Adam and
Eve were originally in the image of God, that is, like God, in this
sense, too. Not only were they created in the natural image of
God in that they were free moral agents, but they were also in his
image in that they had moral excellency, that is, true knowledge,
righteousness, and holiness. Because of the fall, man lost his
moral excellency, while retaining his moral agency. When he
becomes a Christian, the moral excellency of true knowledge,
righteousness, and holiness is renewed within him after the image
of God, who created him. In this second sense, which is peculiar
to Christians, he becomes like God, and therefore is a son of God.

Paul tells us that because God predestined the Christian to be
conformed to the likeness of his Son (Rom. 8:29), the believer is
"transformed into his likeness with ever-increasing glory" (II Cor.
3:18). This means that since Jesus, the natural Son, is like the
Father, and since the Christian, the regenerative son, is like
Jesus, the Christian is also like the Father. In fact, the resemblance between the Christian and God is so great, especially
when contrasted with man's natural state of sin, that Peter, using
a figure of speech, says that Christians "participate in the divine
nature" (II Peter 1:4). He goes on to develop that similarity by
describing the Christians as having escaped "the corruption in
the world caused by evil desires." In virtue of this resemblance,
the Christian is called a son of God.

John alludes to this regenerative sonship of God when he calls
Christians sons of God and then associates this fact closely with
their being as pure as Jesus when he will return from heaven
(I John 3:2). In I John 5:18 he also connects moral purity with
the Christian's sonship when he writes: "We know that anyone

born of God does not continue to sin; the one who was born of God keeps him safe, and the evil one does not touch him."

This is the sonship of God in the regenerative sense. Natural man, who is a son by creation, is made a different kind of son by re-creation, by being born again, born of God. At the new birth he is made holy in principle. He is given a new nature. Thus he is made like God, and because of that similarity can be said to be a regenerative son of God.

It is obvious what the relation of the Holy Spirit is to this regenerative sonship of God. For it is he that establishes it. We are born of the Spirit. This does not mean, of course, that he is our Father, for he is not. The whole Trinity is our Father in this regenerative sense, since we are made like the whole Godhead in our holiness. But it is the third Person in particular who regenerates us and makes us like the Godhead. (See chapter 7 on regeneration.) Jesus, in his conversation with Nicodemus, makes it very clear that we are "born of the Spirit." Therefore, we must be thankful to the Holy Spirit for another kind of sonship of God: not that of Christ nor of the natural man, but one that means that we partake of the divine nature, become brothers of Christ, and are like the Father.

B. *Adoptive Sonship*

There is a second kind of sonship for the Christian in which the Holy Spirit plays an important role, namely, adoptive sonship. This is a great, but often neglected, Biblical theme. As sons of the Reformation we emphasize the glorious theme that we are justified by faith, that is, declared to be righteous in God's sight because Jesus is our substitute. But too often we neglect the equally great doctrine of divine adoption.

Although as unregenerate we may be called sons of God because we are created in his image, yet at the same time we may also be called sons of the devil because of our sin and its results. By nature we are alienated from God and his wrath is upon us. We do not experience his fellowship, nor do we know his love. We tremble in his presence because we know that we are sinful and that he is a just God. We are not the sons of God in the highest, spiritual sense.

But when we become Christians we are not only justified in a legal sense, so that our sins are removed, but we are also adopted as children of God. This is different from regenerative sonship, by which we are made like God in his holiness. Adoption differs from regeneration in much the same way as justification differs from sanctification. Sanctification is an action which occurs within man, making him personally holy. Justification is a transaction which occurs outside of man and does not change his inward nature. It is a legal act by which the Christian is declared to stand in an irreproachable relationship to the law. In a parallel fashion, regeneration is an action that takes place within man at the start of his Christian life, making him inwardly and personally a son of God; whereas adoption is a legal act that occurs outside of man, whereby a son of the devil is declared to be an adopted son of God. That is the difference between the regenerative and adoptive sonship of God.

When that adoptive act takes place, real changes occur in the Christian's relation to God. They are not mere fictive, make-believe changes, as Rome claims them to be, while stressing simply the regenerative sonship within man. But actual changes do occur.

There is, first of all, a change of name from a son of the devil to a son of God. The inheritance is likewise changed. As a son of the devil, a man by divine law must receive his due legacy, which is eternal damnation. As a son of God, however, he inherits eternal life with all of its glory and happiness. For "we are God's children. Now if we are children, then we are heirs— heirs of God and co-heirs with Christ" (Rom. 8:16, 17; Gal. 4:7). Further, the Christian will have care and protection. It will not be like the police protection that a city might give, just and firm, but without love and mercy; but rather it will be like the protection and care that a devoted father will give to his two-year-old. "As a father pities his children, so the Lord pities those who fear him" (Ps. 103:13). The Christian will not fear to go to God because he is a stern, transcendent, righteous God. But he will go freely to him, crying, "Daddy" or "Father," for that is the meaning of the Aramaic "Abba" in Romans 8:15 and Galatians 4:6. "Abba" is the simple, everyday term of a little child for his human father. It may seem irreverent to us, yet it was used by Paul not to indicate irreverence but to show the new filial relationship into which the Christian has entered. For he is "no longer a slave, but a son" (Gal. 4:7). The Christian no longer has to fear God, for God loves him and will care for his every need, as a human father does for his child, only incomparably more wonderfully.

The subject before us now, however, is not adoption, but the Holy Spirit's role in adoption. That role is twofold: first of all, he testifies to us of our adopted sonship, and secondly, he guarantees its continuance.

It is very possible for a person to be a son of God and yet not fully know it. He may be born again, have his sins washed away, be a truly adopted son, and yet doubt his sonship. He may pray: "I do believe; help me overcome my unbelief" (Mark 9:24). Peter presupposed this lack of certainty when he wrote: "Be all the more eager to make your calling and election sure" (II Peter 1:10). John also believed it was possible for a Christian to lack the assurance that he was an adopted child of God, for at the conclusion of his First Epistle, he wrote: "I write these things to you who believe in the name of the Son of God so that you may know that you have eternal life" (5:13). In other words, although John's readers were saved and were sons of God (for they believed, he says), yet they did not know it. They lacked assurance of their salvation.

It is not normal for a Christian to lack assurance, which is an essential part of faith. Yet the fact is that at times that assurance, like a seed, is not fully developed. A person may be a real son of God, entitled to the great privileges of sonship, and yet not realize it. If that is so, he will not have full happiness and peace of mind, because he does not know what the actual facts in his case are.

It is right here that the Holy Spirit assists. For the Holy Spirit causes us to realize that we are adopted sons of God. Without mentioning specifically our sonship, the Scriptures tell us in several places that it is the Holy Spirit who testifies to us about truths in general. Jesus said that the Comforter will testify about Christ (John 15:26; 16:13). John said likewise that "it is the Spirit who testifies, because the Spirit is the truth" (I John 5:6). He cannot lie, he cannot err, for he is the truth; and therefore he testifies to Christians about that truth.

The clearest texts, however, are to be found in Paul's Epistles, where he specifically speaks of this testimony of the Holy Spirit in connection with our sonship. In Galatians 4:6 he says that "God sent the Spirit of his Son into our hearts, the Spirit who calls out, *'Abba,* Father.'" Romans 8:16, 17 is the most explicit of all, for Paul there says expressly: "The Spirit himself testifies with our spirit that we are God's children. Now if we are children, then we are heirs—heirs of God and co-heirs with Christ." It is not exactly clear how the Spirit testifies with our spirits. Does he do it simply by indwelling our hearts, by enlightening our minds? That would be a testimony *to* our spirit. But Romans 8:16 can be translated equally as well as "The Spirit himself testifies *with* our spirit." In other words, alongside of and in addition to his indwelling sanctifying presence, he witnesses along *with* our spirit that we are sons of God.

In the last analysis, however, it makes little difference which interpretation you adopt. In either case, whether he testifies to or with our spirit, the result is the same. We become aware of the fact that we are children of God. We may not be absolutely sure at the start of our sonship or even when we are well along in our new status, yet the Holy Spirit will testify to us in one way or another of the fact of our sonship, and we will receive great joy and comfort. Then we will gradually come into the position of Paul, who had full assurance when he said: "I know whom I have believed; and am convinced that he is able to guard what I have entrusted to him for that day" (II Tim. 1:12); or when he exclaimed at the close of Romans 8 that he was persuaded that *nothing* "will be able to separate us from the love of God that is in Christ Jesus our Lord." We have peace with God. The Holy Spirit assures us that we are the adopted sons of God.

This testimony of the Holy Spirit is the first way in which he has a part in the adoptive sonship of the believer. The second way is by his guaranteeing the continuance of that sonship.

Paul gives to the Ephesians the happy certainty that, having believed on Jesus, they "were marked with a seal, the promised Holy Spirit, who is a deposit guaranteeing our inheritance" (1:13, 14). The word deposit could also be translated as *down payment*. When a person buys a car, for example, he may give a certain part of the total cost of the car to the auto dealer, with the promise to pay the rest later. In the same fashion God gives us a down payment on the inheritance that shall be ours as sons of God. That down payment is the indwelling Holy Spirit, and thereby God assures us that he will give us the rest of our inheritance later on. The Spirit is his promise that, having begun a good work within us, he will continue it until the day of Jesus Christ (Phil. 1:6). The Holy Spirit is God's guarantee that once we are adopted sons, we shall always be his sons, never being snatched out of his hands (John 10:28). And God's down payment is not undependable as is ours. Sometimes we cannot keep up the payments after the initial one is made. We have bitten off too much financially. But not so with God. When he makes the down payment of the Spirit in our lives, he thereby gives an absolute guarantee that the full inheritance will one day come.

In fact, Paul uses another illustration right along with this one of the down payment, when he says that the Ephesians were "marked with a seal" by this down payment. A seal is a means of a person's claiming an object as his and also of making that object secure so that it cannot be lost. Thus, a letter used to be closed with a wax seal and could not be read until the seal was broken. Likewise, Pilate had the stone sealed at the door of Jesus' grave as a security measure against Jesus' body being stolen. In a similar fashion the believer is sealed in his sonship. He is marked as God's and rendered secure from all loss. The Holy Spirit is not only God's down payment for a future inheritance. Paul says that he also acts as a seal by which a believer's security is guaranteed.

This same idea of the Holy Spirit's guaranteeing the continuation of the sonship of the Christian is implied in Romans 8:23, where Paul uses another metaphor, that of the harvest. Here Paul says that the Romans who have the firstfruits of the Spirit are waiting for their adoption, namely, the redemption of their body. The firstfruits were the first crops to be gathered in and were a pledge of a later, abundant harvest. Thus he says that the Romans have within themselves the firstfruits of the Spirit, that is, the Holy Spirit himself. Because they have the Spirit, Paul implies, they will one day have full adoption with all of its inheritance, including the redemption of the body. For as the firstfruits of the harvest are a promise of better things, so the initial possession of the Holy Spirit is a promise of greater things yet to come.

Conclusion

In this sevenfold way we see the richness of the great Biblical concept *son of God* and the necessity of the Spirit in each case, except in Christ's intratrinitarian Sonship. Without the Holy Spirit Jesus could not have been supernaturally born and would not have been called the Son of God by virtue of that birth. Neither would he have lived the moral, religious life of the Son of God. Nor would he have been the Messianic Son of God, winning our salvation for us.

In relation to man, the Holy Spirit was active in the creative sonship in order to give all men a personal likeness to God by creation. If the Holy Spirit had not established this sonship, man would be a brute animal with no capabilities of intellect and imagination.

As far as regenerative sonship is concerned, every believer must give thanks to the Holy Spirit that he is being changed into the image of the Son, and therefore of the Father, with ever-increasing glory, so that, figuratively speaking, he is a partaker of the divine nature.

Finally, may we be grateful to the Spirit for his constant witness to us that we are adopted children of God and that we can run to our heavenly Father and cry, "Abba, Father," making all our wants and wishes known. And may we rejoice that the Spirit is the guarantee, down payment, seal, and firstfruits of the complete spiritual legacy that belongs to us as sons and daughters of God.

The Holy Spirit and Prayer 12

One of the most important aspects of the Christian's life is prayer. Prayer is the communion of the soul with God. By it the Christian worships God, loves him, praises him for his perfections, thanks him for his mercies, confesses his sins to him, asks him for forgiveness, submits to his will, and requests providential and spiritual blessings both for himself and for others.

The Holy Spirit is the mainspring of this prayer life. Therefore, in this chapter we want to see what his work is in our prayers. An understanding of this should enhance our prayers, making them more acceptable to God, as well as more powerful.

We do not propose to study the subject of prayer itself. It would be worthwhile to explain the power of prayer, which is so great that Mary Queen of Scots could say that she feared the prayers of John Knox more than the armies of England. It would be profitable also to set forth the Biblical rules that are prerequisite for effectual prayer. And it would be helpful to study the reasons for unanswered prayer. These subjects, however, are not the direct object of our study. It is rather the relationship of the Holy Spirit to prayer. But as we investigate this one subject, we will also indirectly deal with some of these other problems.

145

I. Prayer in the Holy Spirit

Jesus' disciples once asked, "Lord, teach us to pray." They did not know how. Today we can make that same request, for it is not easy to know how to pray. One essential rule for prayer, however, with many implications, is that we pray "in the Spirit." This phrase is used at least twice in the Bible. Paul told the Ephesians to "pray in the Spirit" (6:18). Jude speaks also of praying in the Holy Spirit (20). In Zechariah we find this same idea, if not the exact phrase, when the prophet, looking forward to the day of Pentecost, prophesied: "And I will pour on the house of David, and on the inhabitants of Jerusalem, the spirit of grace and supplication" (12:10). Zechariah was foretelling the pouring out (to use Joel's Pentecostal terminology) of the Spirit on the Christians at Pentecost. He calls the Holy Spirit the Spirit of grace and supplication. Supplication means asking and requesting, and is a special term for prayer. The prophecy, then, foretold that God would pour out at Pentecost the Spirit of prayer when he poured out the Holy Spirit. To say that Christians have the Spirit of prayer in their lives is essentially the same as saying that they pray in the Spirit. Thus, in effect, these three passages speak of prayer in the Holy Spirit.

But what does it mean to pray "in the Holy Spirit" and to have the Spirit of prayer? First of all, it means that without the Spirit prayer is impossible. It is noteworthy that even the prayer of the unregenerate is prompted by the Holy Spirit. If left to his own sinful inclinations, the man without the indwelling Spirit would curse God and blaspheme. It is obvious that often he does not actively do that. Rather, a Christ-denying Modernist preacher may sometimes offer prayers that seem moving. If he does do so, it is because, without regenerating him or working in him in any saving way, the Holy Spirit restrains him from outward sin and encourages him to outward good, such as prayer. Thus, the Spirit is necessary even in the prayers of the unsaved.

But these prayers are not pleasing in God's sight. They are nothing else than sinful expressions of the unregenerate heart. They are not prayed out of glory to God, nor out of faith. To be sure, prayer by a non-Christian is better than blaspheming and cursing, but without faith in Jesus Christ such prayer lacks the proper motive to make it fundamentally pleasing to God. This type of prayer is not the meaning of Jude's and Paul's expression, "praying in the Spirit."

To pray acceptably to God, to pray with power, one must pray "in the Spirit"; that is, one must be born again and experience the indwelling presence of God. Without the Holy Spirit dwelling in us, God-pleasing prayer cannot be offered. For man is dead spiritually to all good things. He has no spiritual life within him. He does not care to pray to God. He has no desire for it, and therefore he does not pray.

Without life there can be no bodily movement; without life-giving sap there will be no fruit; without fire there can be no heat; and, in a similar fashion, without the Holy Spirit there can be no Christian prayer.

On the other hand, where the Holy Spirit is, there will be power, life, fruit, and actions. For he makes the dead soul alive to God. He creates new desires within it, so that the soul will want to commune with God and will even be unable to resist praying to God. In fact, it is accurate to state if a person does not pray, he is spiritually dead. He is not a Christian. For a person that is "in the Spirit" *must* pray, just as a seed placed in fertile ground and watered must sprout. Where there is life there must be activity. And where the Spirit of prayer is there must be prayer. Thus the first thing to notice about praying "in the Spirit" is that it implies the indwelling presence of the Spirit and, therefore, the desire to pray.

Dwelling within man, the Spirit will then cause him to pray more acceptably to God, not because of a special gift of prayer, but because of his sanctifying influences which have a direct bearing on prayer itself.

For example, the Holy Spirit opens man's eyes to see what he should pray for. Because of sin, man's eyes are closed to truth in general. He cannot see aright. This is particularly true of subjects of prayer. Paul says that "we know not what to pray for" (Rom. 8:26, KJV). When confronted with multiple choices, we do not know which one we should pray for. We find it difficult to apply Scriptural principles to the concrete situations in our lives in order to know what to ask for. At times we do not even understand the Scriptural principles themselves, nor those things which God has clearly revealed we should ask for. If we are to have fruitful prayer, we must know how to pray in accordance with his will. For "we have this assurance in approaching God, that if we ask anything according to his will, he hears us" (I John 5:14). This is one of the secrets of the power of prayer. And one sanctifying function of the Spirit of prayer is to teach us what to pray for so that it may be according to God's will. He enlightens our darkened minds in order that we may see the Biblical principles involved and may apply them aright to our concrete situations.

Praying "in the Spirit" also means that the Spirit will give us the faith that God will hear and answer. This is also essential for fruitful prayer. For God does not hear the ritualistic prayer where the heart is absent. He does not listen to much speaking if there is no trust. Neither are prayers effectual that are simply cried out of distress or intense desire. God does not answer the prayers of those who cry to him in desperation, but who do not think that he will really answer them. Effective prayer must also be accompanied by a belief not only that God *can* answer, but that he *will* do so. That is faith: knowing and trusting. When we pray "in the Spirit," the indwelling Spirit of prayer gives us that faith, so that our prayers conform to this Biblical rule for successful prayer.

Another result of being "in the Spirit" is that we will be increasingly freed from sin. This is important for prayer, too, for as I John 3:22 puts it, we "receive from him anything we ask, because we obey his commands and do what pleases him." And Isaiah said: "Your iniquities have separated between you and your God, and your sins hid his face from you, so that he will not hear" (59:2). Our sins interrupt our communion with God and hinder the answers to our prayers. When the Spirit of prayer comes into our lives, he purifies us and enables us more and more to keep God's commandments. Hence, the Spirit helps the Christian to fulfill this important prayer rule, too.

In summary, to have the Spirit of supplication, or to pray in the Spirit (both of which are synonymous), means to be spiritually enlivened so that we have the desire and ability to pray; to be enlightened in order to know what to pray for so that our requests will be in accordance with the will of God; to have the trust that expects God to answer; and to be enabled to keep God's commandments, a prerequisite for answered prayer. Therefore, first of all, we must pray *in the Spirit.*

II. Prayer by the Holy Spirit

Not only does the Holy Spirit cause *us* to pray, but *he* also prays for us. Not only is there prayer *in* the Holy Spirit, but there is also prayer *by* the Holy Spirit. We find this truth expressed in Romans 8:26, 27.

Here Paul tells us that there is a need for such prayer by the Spirit. He says that we have an infirmity, that is, a weakness, "for we know not what to pray for" (KJV). The Christian does not know his own needs, and therefore he does not know what to pray for.
and therefore he does not know what to pray for.

The Holy Spirit helps out, as we have seen, by enlightening our minds, so that we ourselves are able to pray for the correct things. But he does more than that. In a certain way he also prays for us in our stead. As the text says, "the Spirit himself intercedes for us."

This intercession is not to be confused with Christ's intercession. Christ's intercession occurs in heaven; the Holy Spirit's, on earth. Christ's is outside of our hearts; the Spirit's, within our hearts. Christ intercedes for us in matters of which we may be well aware; the Holy Spirit intercedes for us in matters of which we may not be aware.

There is a difference of opinion how we must conceive of this intercession. Some would say that the Holy Spirit simply stirs up our souls to groanings and desires that are never articulated because they are too deep to be uttered. In other words, he prays *through* us. Others say that the Spirit who dwells within our hearts intercedes by himself, apart from us. He prays for us but not through us, even though he is in us. It is prayer by the Spirit and not by us. In the final analysis it makes little practical difference which interpretation we choose, for the result is the same; in a wonderful way the Holy Spirit fills our need. He prays for us when we should have prayed, but did not know what to pray for.

What a comforting fact! At times we are unaware of dangers ahead, or we do not know which choice we should pray for. We may have a desire to enter two different occupations. We may not know whether to marry a certain girl or not. Two attractive college curricula may appeal to us, but they will lead our lives into vastly different directions. The choice of writing a Christian book or becoming an active church elder may confront us. In them all "we know not what to pray for." Yet the Holy Spirit, knowing exactly what should be prayed for, presents our needs before God.

The marvelous truth is that, because the Spirit intercedes, there will be answered prayer. One reason is, intimates Paul, that God the Father knows what the Spirit is praying. For "he who searches our hearts" (where the Holy Spirit makes his intercessions, whether it be apart from or through us) and is one with the Spirit "knows the mind of the Spirit" (Rom. 8:27).

Furthermore, the Holy Spirit prays according to the will of God. This is always essential for an answer to our prayers, and one reason for unanswered prayers is that we often pray for wrong things, things that are not in accord with the will of God. Sometimes we do this selfishly. Other times we do it in ignorance; we do not know what to pray for. With the Spirit this is different. He searches all things, even the deep things of God (I Cor. 2:10). He is one Person of the Trinity. He knows what is in accord with the will of God. Therefore, as Romans 8:27 expressly says, "The Spirit intercedes for the saints in accordance with God's will." The result is prayer that is always answered because it is in accord with the will of God.

What a wondrous blessing it is to have the third Person of the Godhead making effective intercession for us in important matters of life according to the Father's will! This is prayer *by* the Holy Spirit.

III. Prayer to the Holy Spirit

Now let us examine prayer *to* the Holy Spirit. Sometimes the question is asked. Is it proper to pray to the Spirit alone? This question is tied in with the problem of whom we address in any of our prayers. Do we pray to the Father, that is, to the first Person of the Trinity, or to the Father as the whole Godhead, or to each Person of the Trinity separately? Whom do you have in mind when you pray?

There is little in the Bible that would indicate that when we pray to the Father we are praying to the Godhead as a whole. Rather, the indications point to the first Person of the Trinity. This name, *Father,* is, after all, his title par excellence. Moreover, at times when Jesus spoke of the Father of believers to whom they may go in faith and prayer, he clearly intimated that the Father is the first Person of the Trinity. For example, when he said, "No one comes to the Father except through me" (John 14:6), he obviously excluded himself from the term *Father*. Or when Jesus said to Mary after the resurrection, "I am returning to my Father and your Father" (John 20:17), the close parallel shows that Mary's Father was Jesus' Father, and that he could be none other than the first Person of the Trinity.

Note, too, that in Jesus' farewell discourse, he urged his disciples to pray in his name, but to the Father (John 15:16). It is striking that Jesus did not pray to the Holy Spirit himself for the Spirit's descent at Pentecost, but he prayed to the Father that he would send the Comforter (John 14:16). When we couple this evidence with the observation that Paul prayed almost exclusively to "the God and Father of our Lord Jesus Christ" (thus the first Person of the Trinity), we conclude that one is on good Biblical ground when he directs his prayer chiefly to God the Father of our Lord Jesus Christ, and the Father of all believers.

There are times, however, in which it is proper and even desirable to pray to each Person of the Trinity. Because they sustain special relationships to us and have done special things for us, we should go to them individually.

To the Father we should go, for example, especially when we desire his Fatherly love, care, and protection. To Christ we may pray when we desire to be forgiven for our sins and washed of them. He, after all, died to remove the guilt and stain of sin.

In a similar fashion, it is permissible to pray to the Holy Spirit. If someone, for example, has been bereaved, it is especially to the Holy Spirit that he should go, for it is he chiefly, and not the Father nor the Son, who was sent to be our Comforter. He is the one whose task it is to console us. Or if we recognize a lack of sanctification within ourselves, it is proper to pray to the Spirit to continue to make us holy, for that is one of his prime works in our lives.

So we may pray to the Holy Spirit alone, just as we may pray to each of the other two Persons of the Trinity separately. For examples of excellent prayers to the Holy Spirit, consult the words of numerous hymns on the Holy Spirit found in many a hymnal.

IV. Prayer for the Holy Spirit

Finally, we should not only have prayer in the Spirit, by the Spirit, and to the Spirit, but also, for the Spirit.

We have seen in the preceding chapters how varied the work of the Spirit is, and we still have not concluded our study of him. Some have thought that it was not possible to say much more about the Spirit than what is in the benediction. To the contrary, we have seen that there is much to say about him. His work is many-sided. He has worked wonderful things in the objective world: in creation, in common grace, in the two Words of God. But he also performs wonderful things in the subjective realm. He is the one who regenerates us, makes his abode in us, guides us, testifies to us that we are children of God, seals our inheritance, and is the mainspring of our prayer lives. His work is varied and important for us. For this many-sided work of the Spirit we may certainly pray. In fact, it is our duty to do so.

Let us remember that prayer is a God-given power by means of which we may obtain more of the Holy Spirit. If we desire to have an increased measure of the Spirit—and if we do not receive him more fully, this book has failed in its purpose—we may receive him if we go to God in prayer and ask for him.

If we are confronted with constant sin, then the Holy Spirit is the dynamic that can give us victory over it. If we feel helpless in making life's decisions, then we need the Spirit. If we want greater assurance of our salvation, then the Spirit is the one who can give it to us.

This is also true with prayer. If our prayer life is dull and drab, if it is burdensome and not enjoyable, if we feel out of touch with God, as if our prayers do not reach him, if we do not know what to pray for, if prayer is not a means of power in our lives, then we can go to the Spirit of prayer himself and ask him to come into our lives more fully to help us in this weakness. If we do this in faith with expectation, he will come in and revolutionize our prayer lives. For he is the secret to prayer, just as he is the secret to all holy living. Without him we can do nothing. But with him we can be transformed and can live lives that are spiritually rich, colorful, active, and joyous.

Therefore, pray! Pray in the Spirit, pray to the Spirit, and pray for the Spirit. And the Spirit will pray for you.

The Holy Spirit and the Church 13

After first studying the work of the Spirit in the objective realm, we have given much consideration to his work in the *individual* believer. The Bible goes beyond this atomistic approach, however. It also reveals a corporate work of the Spirit, that is, a work that relates to believers considered collectively. It tells us what the Spirit does, not only in the believer as an individual, but in the church as a whole. It is more than coincidence that the Apostles' Creed confesses that there is a holy, catholic (universal) church and a communion of the saints, immediately after confessing a belief in the Holy Spirit. In this chapter, therefore, we will examine the subject *The Holy Spirit and the Church,* observing successively that the Holy Spirit establishes, unifies, equips, governs, and guides the church.

I. The Holy Spirit Establishes the Church

God has a church on earth that is composed of all true Christians. Not one hypocrite is found in it. It is a spiritual organism of which every true believer is a member, regardless of his affiliation with external organizations. This church is a unit in which all the members are vitally united, so that they are not simply living by themselves and for themselves, apart from others. They are bound together in a real union.

Entrance to this church is by Jesus Christ. He is the door. No one enters the church except by the door. But outside of the door, so to speak, is the Holy Spirit, who sovereignly approaches certain individuals and irresistibly leads them to and through the door, so that they become members of the church of Jesus Christ. In other words, the Holy Spirit establishes Christ's church.

The nature and method of this founding work of the Spirit are readily seen from the Bible. We find that in order to become a part of the church, one must be born again by the Holy Spirit, as Jesus indicated to Nicodemus when he said, "Unless a man is born of water and the Spirit, he cannot enter the kingdom of God" (John 3:5). Every member must also confess that Jesus is Lord, and that can be done only by the Spirit's power. Said Paul, "No one who is speaking by the Spirit of God says, 'Jesus be cursed,' and no one can say, 'Jesus is Lord' except by the Holy Spirit" (I Cor. 12:3). In the same chapter, Paul specifically states that people are united to the church by means of the Spirit. For, in comparing the church to a body, he says: "We were all baptized by one Spirit into one body—whether Jews or Greeks, slave or free—and we were all given the one Spirit to drink" (v. 13). The essential meaning of *to baptize* is *to bring into union*.[1] Thus Paul tells us that whoever we are, we can be in the invisible church only through the Holy Spirit. These passages teach us that it is the Holy Spirit who unites us to the church, of which Christ is the Head. He establishes the church of Christ by regeneration. Just as the Holy Spirit formed the physical body of Jesus Christ in the incarnation, so he also forms the mystical body of Jesus Christ, that is, the church.

It should not be thought, as some contend, that the Spirit founded the church at Pentecost and was not active in the church in the Old Testament period. Stephen spoke of the church as being even in the wilderness (Acts 7:38). Paul said that the Ephesian Gentiles were one with Israel because they were in Christ Jesus (Eph. 2:11-16). And Paul, in commenting infallibly

---

[1] For an excellent treatment of the meaning of baptism, see John Murray's book, *Christian Baptism,* Philadelphia, The Committee on Christian Education, The Orthodox Presbyterian Church, 1952, pp. 4-8.

on Hosea 1, interprets Hosea's references to the Israelites of the Old Testament as applying to the Roman Christians (Rom. 9: 24-26). Thus the church is one in both the Old and New Testaments, and it has always been the Holy Spirit who has introduced new members to the church, whether in the Old or New Testament dispensations.

Since there are no deceiving hypocrites in the mystical body of Jesus Christ, that is, the invisible church of Jesus, and since there is no salvation outside of the invisible church of Christ, each one should ask himself if he has been baptized in a spiritual sense by the Holy Spirit into the body of Christ. Without this baptism there is no salvation.

II. The Holy Spirit Unifies the Church

Not only does the Holy Spirit establish the invisible church of Christ by regenerating men and thus incorporating them into the body of Christ, but he also unifies the church. He does this by dwelling in the church's members. "Don't you know that you yourselves are God's temple and that God's Spirit lives in you?" (I Cor. 3:16). "Do you not know that your body is a temple of the Holy Spirit, who is in you, whom you have received from God?" (I Cor. 6:19). It is by this constant indwelling of the Spirit that members of the church are kept united to Jesus Christ, their Head. The Spirit always mediates the believer's union with Christ; that is, Christ dwells in the believer by means of. or through the Spirit. As Paul said, "If anyone does not have the Spirit of Christ, he does not belong to Christ" (Rom. 8:9). Thus, because the Spirit dwells in the believer, Jesus also comes and dwells in him. In this way each believer becomes a permanent member of the body of Christ and is united to the invisible church.

Not only do believers individually sustain a vital and mystical union with Christ, the Head, but they also sustain a real union with each other. They are not so many individuals, separate from one another and with no connection with each other. Rather, although they are many and different, they are united by the Spirit in such a fashion that together they may be compared to a body, which is composed of various members and yet is a unit. Thus Paul says: "The body is a unit, though it is made up of many parts; and though all its parts are many, they form one body. So it is with Christ. For we were all baptized by one Spirit into one body . . ." (I Cor. 12:12, 13). In Ephesians, using the same illustration, he exhorts his readers "to keep the unity of the Spirit" (4:3), and then says, "there is one body and one Spirit."

In a previous chapter Paul uses another metaphor to illustrate the unity that the Holy Spirit brings to the members of the church. He compares them to building materials that go to make up a temple. As bricks and boards—which by themselves are not related to each other but are separate and disconnected—are brought together to form a beautiful unit, a temple; so also people, who before the indwelling of the Spirit have no basic unity with each other, are united by the indwelling Spirit to form a beautiful temple, the invisible church of Jesus Christ. To use Paul's own words: "In him the whole building is joined together and rises to become a holy temple in the Lord. And in him you too are being built together to become a dwelling in which God lives by his Spirit" (Eph. 2:21, 22).

It is important to notice that this union which the Spirit creates is not simply a union of feeling. It is not merely a matter of love for the other members, an appreciation for them, or a liking of their characteristics. It is not a mental unity, such as may be established even with an unbeliever. But there is a mystical union with the indwelling Spirit that evidently establishes such a real union among believers that Paul does not compare it to some vague mental feeling, but to the relationship that various parts of the body have to each other. Jesus even compares the union of believers to the unity in the Trinity (John 17:11).

This basic unity of believers which the Spirit establishes has a far-reaching implication for the visible church: namely, that wherever possible this underlying, invisible unity should manifest itself in a visible form. Sometimes, out of reaction to the Modernistic church-union movement, orthodoxy goes to the opposite extreme of independentism. Although it would be unscriptural for an Orthodox denomination to unite with a Modernistic denomination, members of the invisible church of Jesus Christ may not *needlessly* and *without good warrant* divide the visible church into separate denominations. To the contrary, denominations must strive to come together, as long as the gospel of Jesus Christ is not compromised. The basic, underlying, spiritual unity should find its expression in the visible church. We should "make

every effort to keep the unity of the Spirit" (Eph. 4:3) and be
one, even as Christ and the Father are one (John 17:11).

III. The Holy Spirit Equips the Church

Although the Spirit establishes a unity in the church, this fact
does not mean that there is uniformity. There can be diversity
in unity, just as an orchestra, composed of violins, French horns,
clarinets, oboes, and drums, can be a composite whole. "There
are different kinds of spiritual gifts, but the same Spirit" (I Cor.
12:4). There are different members, but one body.

Instead of abolishing the distinctive characteristics of each
member, the Holy Spirit establishes them. This is in line with
all of his work. In creating men, he does not make them all the
same, like cars off the same assembly line, but he endows people
with varied gifts, whether physical or mental. In the Old Testament, too, he gave some men special and diverse gifts. To some
he granted artistic skills, to others governing ability, and to others
the gift of judgment. Still others received military wisdom or
courage or physical strength. Even in heaven there will not be a
monotony of uniformity, but a richness of variety.

In a similar fashion, when the Holy Spirit came at Pentecost
to the New Testament church, he gave diverse gifts to the members of that church. To some he granted highly specialized gifts,
such as the gift of tongues, prophesying, miracles, and healings.
These were especially for the New Testament church in its
early history. To others the Spirit granted more ordinary gifts:
the gift of faith or love or hospitality or giving or wisdom or
countless other talents that are found in believers today. In
fact, no one in the true church of Christ is without a gift. For
"to each man the manifestation of the Spirit is given" (I Cor.
12:7).

The Spirit gave these gifts for the profit and welfare of the
church as a whole, and not only for the individual to use and
enjoy for himself. Thus Paul indicates that a nose is very useful
when employed for the other members of the body, but by itself
it is useless. And the talent of the eye is lost unless it is used in
cooperation with the feet, hands, and head (I Cor. 12). The
parts are to be used for the whole.

Paul says this quite pointedly in several places. In I Corinthians
12, which deals entirely with these gifts, he writes that "to each

man the manifestation of the Spirit is given for the common good" (v. 7). In speaking of the gift of tongues, he said that it was better to speak five words with understanding than ten thousand words that could not be understood—the implication being that the church would not profit by it (I Cor. 12:19). "Since you are eager to have spiritual gifts, try to excel in gifts that build up the church" (14:12). In Ephesians Paul says that the giving of gifts is for the perfecting of the saints and the building up of the body of Christ (4:12). They are given to help the other members to become "fullgrown men," growing in the stature of the fullness of Christ.

In this way the Spirit equips the church of Christ. He sovereignly chooses the members from the whole race of man, and then he equips each one with the talents that he knows will be for the welfare of the church as a whole. Unlike the president of the United States, who can only choose his appointees, the Holy Spirit, acting for Jesus, can both appoint the members of the church and endow them with the gifts necessary for their tasks. And this he does absolutely sovereignly, not depending upon us, but giving "them to each man just as he determines" (I Cor. 12:11).

Thus the church is like a temple composed of "living stones" (II Peter 2:5) that have been selected and carefully fashioned. By themselves they are a jumbled pile with no beauty. But chosen and equipped for a special task, they are "built into a spiritual house."

This teaching means that each one who is in the true church of Jesus Christ must be careful to use his gifts for the church. Each and every one has been endowed by the Spirit with some gift for the edification of others. None may say: "I am too old or too weak," or "I am too young or too insignificant." Maybe it is a prominent gift, or perhaps it is not so public. Maybe it is the gift of kindness and helpfulness. Each one, however, has a talent given by the Spirit, and no one may hide it, but must use and develop it. And the Christian is called upon not to use it for his own happiness alone, but to "build up the church" so that it may be "built into a spiritual house."

IV. The Holy Spirit Governs the Church

The church of Jesus Christ has at least two aspects: an invisible

and a visible. What has been said about founding, unifying, and
equipping the church applies to every true member of the
invisible church. But this church also reveals itself in visible
organizations and institutions, such as the Spring Lake Christian
Reformed Church, the Park Street Congregational Church, or
the Hollywood Presbyterian Church. Jesus Christ, through his
apostles, founded the church as an institution. To that church
he gave instructions concerning its task, form of government,
care of the poor, members, discipline, sacraments, and other
similar matters.

Today Jesus, through the Holy Spirit, governs the visible
church as an organization in its various activities. In the first
place, I Corinthians 12:28, as well as Romans 12, indicates that
the Holy Spirit provides human leadership by giving to some to
be apostles, to others prophets, or teachers, or rulers.

Furthermore, in the history of the early church there are
numerous examples of the Holy Spirit guiding and directing the
church. The Holy Spirit told the church at Antioch to ordain
Paul and Barnabas as missionaries (Acts 13:2). To Paul he gave
guidance on his missionary journeys, forbidding him, for instance, to go to a province of Asia Minor, but telling him by a
vision to go to Macedonia (Acts 16:6, 7). He directed the decisions at the Jerusalem council (Acts 15:28) and addressed the
seven churches of Asia Minor (Rev. 2, 3). In many of these
cases, his government was by special revelation in addition to
Holy Scripture, a phenomenon which we do not have at present.
The Holy Spirit does not speak to us today by visions, direct
address, and inspired letters. Yet these examples do indicate that
the Spirit was appointing, directing, and ruling that church, and
we might well expect the same thing to happen today without
such special revelations. We might expect that the Spirit in this
present day sends a certain minister to a certain church, appoints
certain deacons and elders in a specific church at a certain time,
and rules the church in other ways.

This expectation is confirmed by that clear passage in Acts
20:28, where Paul admonishes the Ephesian elders, "Guard
yourselves and all the flock of which the Holy Spirit has made
you overseers. . . ." Although it is true that Jesus is the Head
of the church, and that he appoints his office-bearers, yet, as this
verse indicates, he does it by means of the Holy Spirit. For Paul
says, "the Holy Spirit has made you overseers." Since it is the

Spirit who appoints the elders, and since Christ through the
Spirit is the Head of the whole church in all of its parts, it is
safe to assume that the Spirit also appoints the ministers and
deacons.

This fact is both our comfort and our admonition. It is our
comfort because we know that the office-bearers in a church that
is faithful to God are not elected by the congregation apart from
God. Rather, the Holy Spirit uses the congregation to elect the
men whom he has appointed. He, and not the congregation,
appoints and equips these official representatives of Christ in his
church as an organization. "The Holy Spirit has made you
overseers." Thus it is comforting to know that the church in its
visible, organizational form is governed by the Spirit, and we can
thus be assured that good will come of it.

Yet, God has allowed office-bearers a certain amount of liberty.
They may be sinful and act contrary to his revealed will. That
God does not compel them to be sinless in their governing is
only too obvious. It is just because of this possibility of sinning
that Paul warned the Ephesian elders to guard the flock of
Christ. And to strengthen his exhortation, he reminded them
that, although they were chosen by men, yet it was ultimately
the Holy Spirit who made them elders. Since that was so, their
responsibility was greater, for they were not responsible chiefly
to the Antioch church, but to the Holy Spirit.

Hence we may be comforted today by the fact that the Spirit
governs the church, and therefore the gates of hell cannot prevail
against it. Yet both the congregation and the office-bearers must
remember that just because the Spirit does govern, their responsibility is all the more serious.

V. The Holy Spirit Guides the Church

A final significant activity of the Holy Spirit in connection with
the church is that he guides and directs it into the truth. What
catastrophe would have come upon the church if the Spirit had
not illumined the church's mind, but had allowed it to stumble
along in its sin-caused blindness.

But such is not the case. Christ promised that the Spirit of
truth would guide the church into all truth (John 16:13). And
this has actually happened. Throughout the history of the church
an understanding of the Bible has gradually been developing, so

that today many an untrained church member comprehends more than some of the learned scholars of the early church. For under the guidance of the Spirit, deep theological studies, prolonged discussions, and even sharp controversies have been carried on, sometimes for centuries on one subject, such as the person and natures of Christ. The result has been that by the Spirit's illumination the church has come to accept as obvious, truths of which former church members were not aware.

Thus, the Spirit led the early church to a better understanding of the fact of the Trinity. But it still did not grasp fully the doctrine of the person and natures of Christ. Thereupon the Spirit guided it through long periods of theological controversy, and gradually caused the careful formulation of these truths at important church councils. But even then the church did not comprehend entirely that salvation was by grace alone, and not by any of our works. Under the influence of the Spirit, great men of God, such as Saint Augustine, refuted the Pelagian error of free will and helped the church see the Biblical truth of sovereign grace. Having thus come a long way, the church was still ignorant of other important Biblical facts. But the Holy Spirit, using the study and controversy of men, illumined their minds, so that gradually the church of Jesus Christ came to understand more fully the basic historical truths which we hold today, such as justification by faith, the infallibility of the Bible, the nature of the church, the missionary challenge, eschatology, and even our subject for this book, the doctrine of the Holy Spirit. Due to our sinfulness there are differences of opinion still on many issues, but the fact remains that by and large the Holy Spirit has guided his church into the truth.

Thus, how grateful we must be to the Spirit for this guiding activity. And let no one say: "I do not need doctrine. I'll stick to my Bible." Such an attitude reveals a gross ignorance of the work of the Spirit. For the Holy Spirit has not been working only while we insignificant people of this age read our Bibles or only while one preacher expounds the Scriptures during a sermon. But God has given the gift of the Spirit to the church for thousands of years. During that time he has caused many people from diverse churches and from all lands to understand the Bible better. The result is that through the Spirit's guiding a vast treasure of knowledge has been accumulated in the church of Jesus Christ, so that today the church is incomparably richer than the church in the days of Jesus. To neglect this knowledge is to despise the Spirit of truth. Thus it is the responsibility of each one of us to know to the best of our ability what the Spirit has given us over the centuries. We must study not only the Bible, but also that great storehouse of knowledge which the Spirit has built up over the centuries for the welfare of his whole church and not for the welfare of just a few Christians of a limited period.

Conclusion

To sum up, we see the great work of the Holy Spirit not only in the individual but also in the individuals joined together in the church of Jesus Christ. Under the direction of and for Jesus, the Holy Spirit establishes, unifies, equips, governs, and guides the church. This factor brings assurance and happiness, because the Holy Spirit, being God, most certainly accomplishes his purposes. The devil cannot prevail against the church. But the church will go down through the centuries governed and guided by the Spirit, so that it will be exactly the type of church that Jesus wants it to be.

At the same time, this places responsibilities on us all. When we realize that it is the Holy Spirit who establishes the church, then we must ask ourselves: Have we been born again, born of the Spirit, born into the invisible church of Jesus Christ, outside of which there is no salvation?

Because the Spirit brings the members of Christ's church into that mystical union with Christ and with each other, it is the duty of each of us to see to it that we do not disrupt that unity in the visible realm. We may not be bickering and fighting among ourselves in the same church, and we should seek organizational unity with all true members of Christ's church, even those outside of our denomination, if that can be accomplished without compromise of our principles.

Because the Spirit equips every member of Christ's church with certain gifts or talents, it is obligatory for every Christian to find out what those gifts are and then to employ them for the benefit of the church.

Since the elders, deacons, and ministers of this church are appointed by the Holy Spirit to their respective offices, each one must realize the gravity of the situation and attempt to put forth more effort to discharge his duties well.

Finally, since the Spirit has guided his church from its inception, it is mandatory that each one study his Bible in the light of this vast accumulation of knowledge that the Spirit has given his church.

Because of the Spirit's work in the church, there are not only blessings but also solemn duties for its members. May the Holy Spirit guide each one of us in fulfilling them.

The Holy Spirit *and* His Symbols

14

Down-to-earth illustrations can often clarify hard-to-understand subjects. Thus Jesus compared himself to a door, a street, a piece of bread, and a cup of water. He likened the kingdom of God to a pearl, a fish net, a supper, a tree, a seed, and a hidden treasure. Paul illustrated his deep theology with references to stars, the foundation of a house, the parts of a body, light and darkness, hay, and jewels.

Likewise, it is possible to make the truths concerning the Holy Spirit more intelligible to us earthbound mortals. He is an invisible Spirit and an incomprehensible God, and for these reasons it is difficult to define his person and his work. But God knows our weaknesses, and therefore in his Word he employs symbols, that is, visible signs for an invisible reality. The Bible compares the Holy Spirit to water, wind, breath, fire, oil, a dove, a fruit tree, a down payment, and a seal. By observing the Biblical use of these symbols, it is possible to come to a riper insight into many aspects of the work of the Spirit of God.

I. Water

In several places the Bible closely associates the Holy Spirit

165

with water. It does so for two purposes: first, to indicate that the
Holy Spirit cleanses the Christian spiritually; and, second, to
indicate that he is the source of life.

Even children can understand both of these illustrations. We
know only too well how children can play outside and get muddy.
They can, intentionally or unintentionally, smear the mud on
their pants, on their faces, and in their hair. But we know, too,
that there is one remedy for dirt, that is, water. It will remove
the mud from their clothes, face, and hair, so that all that was
dirty will be sparkling clean—for a while, at least.

This is the imagery which the Bible uses of the regenerating
work of the Holy Spirit. It portrays man as being figuratively
dirty, filthy, and polluted because of his sins. But when the
Spirit comes into a person's life, he cleanses it from its sin. He
regenerates the heart and sanctifies the life, so that gradually the
polluting sin is conquered and eventually eliminated. In this
sense man is cleansed and purified from his sins, just as the dirty
hands and clothes of a little boy are cleansed by water.

Thus Jesus told Nicodemus, "Unless a man is born of water
and the Spirit, he cannot enter into the kingdom of God" (John
3:5). It is not easy to determine the meaning of the word *water*
in this instance. It may be a direct emblem of *Spirit*. Or it may
be a symbol of baptism, which is by water. In the latter case, it
would indicate the purification that is signified in baptism, the
purification from our sins by the indwelling Spirit. In either
case, water is closely associated with the Spirit. And Jesus' meaning is that in order to enter into the kingdom of heaven we must
be born of the Spirit, who cleanses us from our sins just as water
washes away dirt.

This same idea is hinted at in Psalm 51, when David prays:
"Wash me and I will be whiter than snow. . . . Create in me a
clean heart, O God. . . . Renew a right spirit within me . . .
and take not your Holy Spirit from me." Ezekiel uses the same
figure of speech when he writes: "And I will sprinkle clean water
upon you, and you will be clean: from all your filthiness, and
from all your idols, will I cleanse you. . . . And I will put my
Spirit within you" (36:25-27). And Paul makes a definite reference to the cleansing power of the Spirit through regeneration
when, in writing to Titus, he says that God "saved us, through
the washing of rebirth and renewal by the Spirit" (3:5). The
parallel use of *water* and *the Spirit* in these three passages illus-

trates to us the cleansing power of the regenerating and sanctifying Spirit.

Water is not only useful to cleanse away dirt, but it is also necessary for life, whether it be human, animal, or vegetable.

A good spring can bubble forth an abundance of water, so that even after buckets of water have been drawn, the well is still overflowing. A spring on higher ground, as it spills over and downward, will cause greenness and life wherever it goes. In fact, it can turn a dead, barren desert into an oasis, or into the productive banks of the Nile, or into the lushness of southern California.

Using this easily observed fact, the Bible describes the Spirit and his influences. Jesus said: "If a man is thirsty, let him come to me and drink. Whoever believes in me, as the Scripture has said, streams of living water will flow from within him. By this he meant the Spirit" (John 7:37-39). That means that the believer will have a life of holiness that will be like rivers of living water. But those rivers of good works have a source, namely, the Holy Spirit. He is "the spring of water welling up to everlasting life," as Jesus put it elsewhere (John 4:14). When one believes on Jesus, the Holy Spirit abides in his life and causes him to live a life of holiness. The Spirit acts as a fountain within the Christian, from which flow rivers of good works, going out to others. The Holy Spirit produces life.

This is also the meaning of Isaiah when he quotes God as saying: "For I will pour water on him that is thirsty, and streams on the dry ground; I will pour my Spirit on your seed, and my blessing on your offspring; and they will spring up among the grass, as willows by the water courses" (Isa. 44:3, 4). Wherever the Spirit comes, there comes life also. He is to a dead soul what water is to desert soil. He produces spiritual life, just as water gives physical life to thirsty, dry ground.

Thus water describes a twofold activity of the Spirit: his cleansing and life-giving power. We should ask ourselves if we know the Spirit of God as water. Are we being cleansed by him from our sinful habits, and is he a fountain to our souls, causing us to bring forth rivers of holiness?

II. Wind

In Jesus' discourse with Nicodemus, he compares the Spirit not only to water, but also to the wind. "The wind blows wherever it pleases. You may hear the sound, but you cannot tell where it comes from or where it is going. So it is with everyone born of the Spirit" (John 3:8).

The symbolism is clear. First of all, the way in which the Spirit works in regeneration is mysterious. It cannot be thoroughly understood. He and his operations are invisible. As is the case with the wind, one can see the results, but not the actual activity that causes the results. A hurricane rushes toward an island in the Pacific. It moves hundreds of tons of water into mountainous waves. The sterns of great ships are lifted out of water only to spank the water as they descend. Trees are bent and uprooted. Roofs of houses are torn off. The results of the storm are very evident. But no one has ever seen the wind that causes them. It is invisible. So also is the Spirit, said Jesus. One can see the results of the Spirit's work: holiness, good works, and powerful lives; but one can never see the Holy Spirit. He is just like the wind.

The reception of the Spirit at Pentecost illustrates this same point. That he was there is clear, for the apostles spoke in tongues and performed many signs and wonders. But the Spirit could not be seen. Rather, there was only a symbol of him: "a sound like the blowing of a violent wind" (Acts 2:2). God used the wind as an emblem of the Spirit to indicate, among other things, his invisibility.

A second meaning of the symbol *wind* is power. A hurricane, a typhoon, and a tornado reveal tremendous force, although any wind has some degree of power. So it is with the Holy Spirit. Man stubbornly fights against God. He will have nothing to do with the Savior. Other men cannot persuade him with logic or eloquence. Power is necessary to affect his life. And the Holy Spirit has that power, just as wind has power. When he comes into a sinner's life, he brings about radical changes. He penetrates into the innermost recesses of the sinner's heart, and with a powerful, efficacious, and irresistible force, he softens his hardened heart and turns him crying to Jesus. The Spirit is as powerful as a hurricane driving a craft before it. Therefore he is symbolized at Pentecost as "the blowing of a violent wind" (Acts 2:2).

This emblem of the Spirit, the wind, also reveals the complete sovereignty of the Spirit. Meteorologists can describe winds, trace them after they have blown their course, measure their velocities, find out their devastating power, and even predict their course with some degree of accuracy. But they cannot control them. They cannot lift a tornado up into the air as it approaches a city, or turn a hurricane that is heading for Florida back into the Atlantic, or slow down a typhoon as it draws near a South Sea island. The wind is absolutely sovereign. It "blows wherever it pleases" (John 3:8). So also is the Holy Spirit. He regenerates whom he desires, when he desires. No one can control his activity nor dictate to him where he shall go or what he shall do. He is sovereign.

The realization of the meaning of this emblem of the Spirit should cause each one who is regenerated to thank God for the mysterious, powerful, and sovereign working of the Spirit in his life, whereby the Spirit subdued the stubborn rejection of Christ in his heart.

III. Breath

Very closely related to the symbol of wind is the symbol of breath for the Holy Spirit. In fact, in both Hebrew and Greek the one word can be translated in three different ways: as wind, breath, and the Spirit, thereby showing their close interrelationship.

Just as wind is an appropriate symbol for the Spirit of God because it is invisible, so is breath a fitting sign because it, too, is invisible. But the word *breath* implies something else besides the invisibility of the Holy Spirit. It is something that comes from inside a person and indicates that there is life within him. When a person dies, we sometimes say: "There is no more breath in him. He is dead." Or, as the psalmist says of animals, "You take away their breath, they die, and return to dust" (Ps. 104:29). In this sense, breath is used in the Bible as a symbol of the Spirit. It points to the fact that the Spirit is life-giving.

The Bible uses this emblem to show that the Spirit gives life in four different ways. It denotes, first of all, that the Spirit gives natural life. In Genesis 2:7, with a direct allusion to the Spirit, the Scriptures speak of the giving of life to man by saying that God "breathed into his nostrils the breath of life." And in Job 33:4 Elihu says, "The Spirit of God has made me, and the breath [symbol for the Spirit] of the Almighty gives me life."

In addition to natural life, the Spirit also gives spiritual life. By regeneration he spiritually enlivens those who are dead in sins and trespasses. In this activity, too, the emblem of breath is used to signify the Spirit. In Ezekiel's vision of the dry bones, there is not only a prophecy of the restoration of Israel's political, national life, but also a direct reference to spiritual renovation of individuals. For we read: "Prophesy, son of man, and say to the wind, Thus says the Lord GOD: Come from the four winds, O breath [this is the symbol for the Holy Spirit], and breathe upon these slain that they may live. So I prophesied as he commanded me, and the breath came into them, and they lived, and stood up on their feet, an exceeding great army" (Ezek. 37:9, 10). Thus breath indicates the Spirit as he regenerates souls that were dead to God.

There is a third way in which this symbol of breath depicts the life-giving activity of the Spirit. After the resurrection, when Jesus appeared to the disciples behind closed doors, "He breathed on them, and said, 'Receive the Holy Spirit'" (John 20:22). His physical breathing did not give the disciples the Holy Spirit, but it was symbolic of it. Because of the whole context, we see that this giving of the Spirit was not for sanctifying purposes—that was to come at Pentecost when three thousand were converted—but so that the disciples would be equipped to perform their official duties as apostles: to forgive and to retain sins by the preaching of the Word and by church discipline (v. 23). Hence, in this passage, breathing symbolized the giving of the Spirit for the life and power of the official ministry of the disciples, as office-bearers in the church of Christ.

A fourth sense in which breath is used to symbolize the life-giving qualities of the Spirit is in connection with the inspiration of the Bible. In the classical text to prove the inspiration of the Word of God, Paul says that "all Scripture is God-breathed" (II Tim. 3:16). *God-breathed* is an exact translation of the Greek, which is usually translated as *inspired by God*. To say that the Scriptures are God-breathed (inspired) instead of simply God-made or God-created is a direct allusion to the breathing work of the Holy Spirit in inspiration. For even as the etymology of the word *inspire* (that is, *inbreathe*) implies, the Holy Spirit breathed into the Bible authors, inspiring them to write the Bible without error. He gave them life, as it were, for this special task. He acted as the breath of God as he produced God-breathed Scriptures. Therefore, in this fourth sense, too, breath is a fitting symbol of the Spirit of God.

Thus when you think of the Scriptural symbol of breath, remember not only the Holy Spirit's invisible but also his life-giving activity in the creation of natural man, in the re-creation of spiritual man, in the bestowing of life and power for official apostolic tasks, and in the inspiration of the Bible. And ask yourself: Do I experience the Spirit as breath? Do I know his life-giving qualities in regeneration? and, Have I, if I am an office-bearer, been equipped for my tasks by the breathing of the Holy Spirit upon me?

IV. Fire

Everyone understands the symbol of fire. Fire is power. Its power can be seen as it transforms a gasoline storage tank into a flaming inferno, as towering trees burn to blackened skeletons, as buildings are toppled, or a whole city block is gutted. It is evidenced in huge engines which are driven by steam that has been produced by fire. Figuratively speaking, we talk of setting the world afire with an ideology. All are aroused for a certain project or goal: they are on fire. So fire is power.

It is in this sense that fire seems to be used as an emblem of the Spirit. At Pentecost, when the Spirit descended, there was not only a symbol in the "sound like the blowing of a violent wind," but there was also another symbol in "what seemed to be tongues of fire" that came to rest on the heads of each one in the house (Acts 2:3). This was symbolic of the new power that came to the church by the Spirit on that day, just as Jesus had prophesied earlier, "But you will receive power, when the Holy Spirit comes on you." Because of that power of the Spirit, because disciples were on fire with the Spirit, they became Christ's "witnesses in Jerusalem, and in all Judea and Samaria, and to the ends of the earth" (Acts 1:8).

Fire is also a purifying force. The Bible frequently uses the illustration of refining metals by fire. Metal ore was put into a refiner's fire, and through the intense heat the dross and impurities were burned off, so that only metals of the finest and purest qualities remained. In a similar way, the Holy Spirit acts as fire, purifying sin from the believer's life. He convicts of sin and pricks the conscience, so that the old sins are burned off, and gradually a purer specimen of holiness is obtained.

This may well be the meaning of the tongues of fire which symbolized the Holy Spirit at Pentecost, and of Jesus' statement, "I have come to bring fire on the earth" (Luke 12:49); and of John the Baptist's remark, probably referring to Pentecost, when he said that he baptized only with water, "but after me will come one who . . . will baptize you with the Holy Spirit and with fire" (Matt. 3:11).

It would be well to ask ourselves if we have been baptized with the Spirit of fire. Are we energized, so that we do things for the kingdom? Have we received power, so that we are witnesses in Jerusalem, and in all Judea and Samaria, and to the ends of the earth? Do we experience the power of the Spirit as a refining influence which consumes the sins in our lives? Do we dwell in sin? Or have we gained the victory that can come only by the Spirit of power and purification? If not, we should go to the Spirit of fire.

V. Oil

A fifth emblem of the Holy Spirit is oil. The symbolism must be derived from those several passages in the Old Testament that speak of anointings, and from the anointing of Christ and the Christian with oil in the New Testament. In Old Testament times it was a practice to anoint the prophets, priests, and kings. This was done by pouring oil on their heads, and this anointing symbolized their appointment to office and the giving of the Spirit to qualify them for their work. Therefore, oil was a symbol of the Spirit of God.

This idea of anointing was carried over from the Old Testament Hebrew to the New Testament Greek and is found in Jesus' title, *Christ. Christ* means the *Anointed One.* Just as the anointed ones were prophets, priests, and kings in the Old Testament, so Jesus was par excellence *the* Prophet, *the* Priest, and *the* King. All the Old Testament offices converged on him. To this threefold office he was anointed at his baptism, when the Spirit descended in the form of a dove. Immediately afterward, he entered into his public, official ministry of preaching and performing miracles. And in his first sermon he quoted Isaiah 61, saying, "The Spirit of the Lord is on me, therefore he has anointed me to preach good news to the poor" (Luke 4:18). Thus the Spirit is compared to oil, and the anointing symbolizes the coming of the Spirit into Christ to equip him as the Messianic Son of God for his threefold task.

This same symbolism is applied to the Christian. The very word *Christian* is derived from the name *Christ,* and indicates that Christians are anointed ones, just as Christ is the Anointed One. And that is true. Christians are anointed by the Holy Spirit. To be sure, it is not the special anointing of the Old Testament prophets or priests or kings; nor is it the anointing that was unique with Jesus. But every believer is a prophet, priest, and king in a general sense. Peter intimates this when he calls Christians "a royal priesthood, a holy nation" (I Peter 2:9). John even uses the word *anointing:* "But you have an anointing from the Holy One, and all of you know the truth" (I John 2:20). And Paul writes that God "anointed us" (II Cor. 1:21).

We see, then, figuratively speaking, that the Holy Spirit is the oil of anointing. He equipped the office-bearers of the Old Testament to perform their duties. He qualified Christ in his threefold task. And he anoints the Christians today, giving them spiritual gifts as prophets, priests, and kings. He anoints them as prophets so that their minds are illumined to understand God's Word, and so that they may tell others. He anoints them as priests by sanctifying them so that they can offer up spiritual sacrifices to God. And the Spirit of oil anoints them as kings so that they may reign, as kings, over every form of sin.

VI. Dove

All four Gospels describe the Holy Spirit as descending "like a dove" on Jesus at his baptism. The only other instance of the Spirit appearing in the figure of a bird is Genesis 1:2, where we read that he was brooding over the face of the waters. This suggests the picture of a bird brooding over eggs in a nest.

The Bible does not tell us why the Spirit descended on Jesus in the form of a dove, rather than of some other bird or object. We do know that the dove is the symbol of purity, gentleness, harmlessness, and tenderness. Jesus was to say later on: "I am sending you out like sheep among wolves. Therefore be as shrewd as snakes and as innocent as doves" (Matt. 10:16). We know that Jesus was the embodiment of gentleness and meekness. He said of himself, "I am gentle and humble in heart" (Matt. 11:28). Paul pleaded with the Corinthians "by the meekness and gentleness of Christ" (II Cor. 10:1). His whole life was one of kindness, love, concern for others, and absence of harshness.

Therefore, to see the Spirit descend as a dove on him would call these characteristics to mind. It is a reminder for us today that no one needs to fear to go to Jesus, for he is full of kindness, gentleness, and love. He invites all who are weary and burdened to come to him and they will find rest for their souls.

VII. The Fruit Tree

Although Jesus once compared the Christian to a fruit tree (Matt. 7:16 ff.), Galatians 5:22 uses the metaphor in describing the Holy Spirit. Paul's point is that the unregenerated person brings forth fornication, uncleanness, lasciviousness, and the other sins mentioned in verses 19-21; but that, just as a fruit tree produces fruit, so also the Holy Spirit produces in man such good virtues as love, joy, peace, and patience.

If we do not have that fruit, may we be warned, because Jesus told us in a parable that we will be cut off, since without fruit we are worthless. "Cut it down! Why should it use up the soil?" (Luke 13:7). Elsewhere he said that the Father "cuts off every branch in me that bears no fruit" (John 15:2) and "such branches are picked up, thrown into the fire and burned" (v. 6).

Conclusion

Other symbols of the Spirit could be mentioned, such as the seal, the down payment, and the firstfruits of the harvest. But since we have dealt with these in chapter 11, we refer the reader to the treatment of them there.

May, then, this symbolic language concerning the Spirit remain vivid in our memories. If we want to know cleansing from sin in our lives, as well as spiritual growth, then we must know the Spirit as symbolized by water. If we would understand something of the mysteriousness, power, and sovereignty of the Spirit's working in our lives, then we must think of the wind. If we would experience spiritual quickening, and if the office-bearers of a church would be made alive and equipped for their church duties, then we must understand the symbolism of the Spirit as breath. To realize the power and purification that comes by the Spirit, let us think of fire. If we want to be equipped for the threefold task of an anointed Christian, we should meditate on the symbolic meaning of anointment with oil. If we are looking for a Savior who is full of love and gentleness and purity, we should ponder the Spirit's descending on him in the form of a dove. If we would live a holy life, we must contemplate the meaning of the Spirit as a fruit tree producing fruit.

God has given us these symbols in his Word for a purpose—that we may understand more clearly the fullness of the indwelling of the Spirit in our lives. May this fuller understanding enrich our spiritual lives.

The Holy Spirit and the Unpardonable Sin

15

There is a sin God will never forgive.

All other sins may be pardoned, regardless of how heinous they are or how often they have been committed. Although God is holy and righteous, he is also a God of love. He sent his Son to bear the torments of hell as a substitute for sinners. He pleads with sinners to repent. The sinner's confidence is that God will forgive all sins repeatedly for Christ's sake—except one.

Every sin and blasphemy may be forgiven men, but the blasphemy against the Spirit will not be forgiven (Matt. 12:31). If any reader of these lines commits this sin, he can never be saved. He will never have a second chance. He may read the Bible or hear the gospel preached, but entrance to heaven is eternally closed to him. It is too late. God will never pardon. The whole church may pray for him, but it will never help because he has sinned a sin that leads to death (I John 5:16). As a matter of fact, the church should not even pray for such a person (I John 5:16). According to Jesus, he "is guilty of an eternal sin" (Mark 3:29) and will never find forgiveness. Therefore, it is important for everyone to know what the Bible says about this one unpardonable sin, this sin against the Holy Spirit.

177

I. What It Is Not

A. Final Unbelief

Sometimes it is stated that the only sin God does not forgive is unbelief at death. God will pardon all other transgressions, it is said, except the failure to trust in Christ for forgiveness.

It is true that there is no second chance after death and that if a person dies without believing, he will be lost forever. In a sense this failure to believe may be called an unpardonable sin, too. But what is usually called the unpardonable sin is a sin that is committed some time before death—maybe a long time before. When Jesus spoke about this sin—although he did not call it the unpardonable sin—he alluded to Pharisees, who were not on the point of death (Matt. 12:32; Mark 3:29; Luke 12:10). When Hebrews 6:6 says that it is impossible to renew some again unto repentance, the implication is that the unpardonable sin is not a death-bed one, but one that may occur well before that time.

B. Denial of Christ

Some think that if a person, being confronted with a powerful and clear presentation of the gospel, such as at an evangelistic meeting, rejects the gospel offer, then he has blasphemed the Holy Spirit and may never be saved.

But this is unscriptural, as can be seen from the conversion of former Christ-deniers such as Paul (Acts 26:9; I Tim. 1:13), the brothers of Christ (Mark 3:21; John 7:5), and the Jewish priests who were converted in Stephen's day (Acts 6:7). Furthermore, Peter denied Christ three times, and yet Christ forgave him after the resurrection. Moreover, in the very discourse on the unpardonable sin, Christ said that "everyone who speaks a word against the Son of man will be forgiven" (Luke 12:10). Blasphemy against the Spirit is not the doubting of unbelievers. nor even the usual reasoned denial of Christ and of God in general. An atheist has not necessarily committed the unpardonable sin. Christ-deniers at times do turn to Christ and are forgiven. People who have denied Christ in the past should not be frightened by this supposition, provided they now look to Christ for salvation.

C. Denial of the Deity of the Holy Spirit

At first blush Jesus, in Matthew 12:32 and Luke 12:9, 10,

seems to be warning against the denial of the deity of the Holy Spirit or against the profane, frivolous, light use of the Spirit's name in swearing. He delineates the sin as "speaking against" (Matt.) and "blaspheming" (Luke) the Holy Spirit. Although such swearing is a serious sin, yet, as will be seen from Hebrews 6:4-6, denial of the Spirit's Godhead and the frivolous use of his name do not constitute this sin and such sins may be forgiven.

D. Grieving the Holy Spirit

It is possible for Christians to sin against their better knowledge. David clearly understood the Sixth and Seventh Commandments, yet he murdered Uriah and committed adultery with Bathsheba. Paul against better wisdom did things that he knew he should not have done (Rom. 7). And what Christian has not experienced wicked and even blasphemous thoughts, which he knows are wrong and which go against his better judgment? Paul warned against such conscious sinning when he admonished the Ephesians not to "grieve the Holy Spirit of God" (Eph. 4:30) and when he charged the Thessalonians not to "put out the Spirit's fire" (I Thess. 5:19). Similar resisting[1] of the Holy Spirit, some suggest, is the essence of the unpardonable sin.

Yet, if some Christians have resisted the Spirit of God, they should not fear that they have necessarily blasphemed against the Holy Spirit and will never be able to go to heaven. In spite of having grieved the Holy Spirit, David was a child of God; Paul could later cry, "Abba, Father"; the Ephesians were foreordained unto adoption (Eph. 1:5); and the Thessalonians were elect (I Thess. 1:4). These saints who had grieved the Holy Spirit were not eternally lost. It is a grievous thing for a Christian to resist the operations of the Holy Spirit; yet, it would be misleading and unbiblical to claim that such a sin is the heart of the blasphemy against the Holy Spirit.

E. Falling Away of the Saved

Hebrews 6:4-5 states that those who have committed the unpardonable sin have been enlightened, tasted the heavenly gift,

[1] Acts 7:51 uses the word "resist" in reference to stubborn Jews.

shared in the Holy Spirit, and tasted the goodness of the word of God. At first glance it might seem that the author is speaking of Christians and that the nature of the "eternal sin" (Mark 3:29) is final and complete backsliding. In other words, some were saved, but they disbelieved, fell away, and ceased to be Christians.

Because some Christians have deprived themselves of great peace out of fear that they have committed this sin, it is necessary to state emphatically that Christians cannot blaspheme against the Holy Spirit. The grand truth of the Bible is: Once saved, always saved. God is not fickle, ceasing to finish what he began (regeneration), but Paul is "confident of this, that he who began a good work in you will carry it on to completion until the day of Christ Jesus" (Phil. 1:6).

In John 10:27-30 Jesus gives us one of the strongest affirmations that Christians can never be lost. In the first place, he says that he gives *eternal* life to his sheep, i.e., those who believe in him. If a person has eternal life, he can never fall away. If he could, he would not have eternal life, but only temporary life. Then the text would read: "I give unto them temporary life." Yet Jesus expressly describes the Christian's life as being eternal. Secondly, Jesus says that "they shall never perish." This is a direct contradiction of Hebrews 6:4-6, if that passage is interpreted to mean that Christians can perish. Thirdly, Jesus makes the sweeping statement that "no one can snatch them out of my hand." No one—a third party, the devil or the Christian himself—is able to cause a lamb of Christ to be lost. The reason is that the Father gave the sheep to the Son, and the Father is greater than all. Therefore, "no one can snatch them out of my Father's hand."

Because of the repeated testimony of the Bible to the permanence of salvation and because the Bible never contradicts itself, it is impossible to interpret Hebrews 6 as referring to the saved who have become "unsaved." It is important to underscore that the unpardonable sin is not a final falling away of Christians. Christians cannot commit the unpardonable sin.

II. What It Is

Although the blasphemer against the Holy Spirit is not a Christian, he is one in whom the Holy Spirit has been working, though

in a non-saving way. Hebrews 6:4, 5 gives the best description
of the blasphemer and his sin. It describes him in six ways:

A. Enlightened

The New Testament uses this figure of speech in the same
way that modern man does, applying it to knowledge. The
natural man is blind to spiritual truths, his understanding is
darkened, and he cannot comprehend the things of the Spirit
of God.[2] When he is born again, the Bible says that his eyes
are opened and his mind illumined, so that he has a basic knowledge of truth. In the case of the unpardonable sin, however,
man is enlightened without experiencing the regenerating,
saving influence of the Holy Spirit. Hebrews 10:26 says that he
received a knowledge of the truth.

The Bible does not describe this enlightenment further. But
the occasion of Jesus' remarks on the blasphemy against the
Spirit is instructive at this point. Jesus had performed great
miracles in the presence of the Pharisees. He had healed a man
by ejecting a devil, causing him to see and giving him his
speech. The Godhead of Christ was so plainly visible that "all
the people were astonished and said, 'Could this be the Son of
David?' " (Matt. 12:23). This clear knowledge of Christ was
part of the enlightenment of the Pharisees who were blasphemers
of the Holy Spirit.

Judas is another example. He was enlightened by Jesus'
presence and conversations and probably he experienced the
power of the Holy Spirit in performing miracles with the other
disciples. Yet, he openly renounced his Lord. Balaam, too,
probably committed this sin by turning in hate against God.
Yet he was enlightened so that he even prophesied about the
future Messiah. If King Saul and Caiaphas are other examples
of those who committed this sin, it is noteworthy that they, too,
were enlightened by the Spirit.

B. Tasted of the Heavenly Gift

The gift is the life and work of Christ. It was not of the
earth, but heavenly, i.e., it had a heavenly nature and a heavenly
source. The guilty parties had actually tasted him. They had

---

[2] See chapter 5, "The Holy Spirit & Illumination," pp. 53-61.

not simply heard about him, but from firsthand experience had
seen him, seen him work, and heard him teach. They did not
feast on Christ in true communion, but they did taste in that
they had a personal experience with him. It was this firsthand
knowledge that aggravated the sin so greatly.

C. Sharers in the Holy Spirit

This cannot mean that the guilty ones were indwelt by the
Holy Spirit so that they were mystically united to Christ as the
branches are to the vine (John 15). For this is true of the
saved only, and, as we have seen, those who have committed the
unpardonable sin are not Christians.

Probably this sharing refers to the sharing in the work and influence of the Spirit. The Holy Spirit worked in miraculous and
prophetic ways even through unbelievers. Unregenerate Balaam,
Saul, and Judas are examples of men in whom the Spirit worked.
Jesus also indicated that unbelievers share in the Spirit in this
sense when he prophesied that many will say: "Lord, Lord, did
we not prophesy in your name, and in your name drive out
demons and perform many miracles?" (Matt. 7:22). And yet he
will tell them that he never knew them. Even the intellectual
but nonsaving illumination may be considered as a part of the
sharing of the Holy Spirit.

D. Tasted the Goodness of the Word of God

The person who commits the unpardonable sin has tasted the
goodness of the word of God. The emphasis here is on the word
goodness. The thought is essentially that he has found that the
Word of God—the gospel—is good. His heart is warmed at the
news of salvation. He does not eat of it fully, but tastes it. Yet
his heart rejoices at it. He is like the seed that fell on rocky
soil. He receives the Word quickly and with joy, but stumbles
when persecution comes (Mark 4:16, 17). He is like King
Herod, who heard John gladly (Mark 6:20) and yet rejected
his message of Christ. He tastes that it is good, but does not
really eat.

E. Tasted the Powers of the Coming Age

The word *powers* is used in Hebrews 2:4 in reference to

miracles, and may have that meaning here. This would then be a repetition of thoughts already mentioned.

F. Fell Away

In spite of this lucid knowledge and experience, the blasphemers renounced Christ. Not in the usual doubting or ordinary unbelief; nor reluctantly against their will as Paul sinned (Rom. 7); nor with any sadness or compunction such as Peter felt after he denounced Christ; but deliberately (Heb. 10:26).

The clearest example of this blasphemy is the rejection of Christ by the Pharisees on the occasion already mentioned in the Gospels. The Pharisees had clearly seen God Almighty with their own eyes—they had heard him and touched him. They saw him teach as no mortal could. They had watched him do miracles many times. Now they saw him perform three miracles in one person: restoring sight, granting speech, and ejecting a demonic spirit. Yet they refused to admit that he was God. Instead, so filled with brazen, hateful venom were they, they not only denied that he was God, but they accused him who had just cast out a devil of being a devil himself. They made God Satan, and Satan God. It was a devilish revolution against God.

This same sin can happen today as it did in Biblical times. Although the age of miracles has passed, it is possible for modern man, enlightened by the Spirit of God and tasting that the Word of God is good, to rebel against Christ openly, brazenly, and without any remorse. This is especially true of those who have been reared in orthodox Christian homes and churches where they have heard the gospel fully, plainly, and properly over the years. It is possible for them to be warmed by the clear presentation of the Gospel and then willfully, hatefully, and openly to renounce Christ completely.

III. The Punishment

The results of such blasphemy are tragic. Such sinners can never be saved. They will never have another opportunity to believe. "It is impossible for those . . . to be brought back to repentance" (Heb. 6:4-6), to be enlightened or moved by the Spirit as they once were. Just because they saw, tasted, and experienced the heavenly gifts, their damnation will be the greater. "Anyone who speaks against the Holy Spirit will not be forgiven, either in this age or in the age to come" (Matt. 12:32). For it is "a sin that leads to death," for which no church should pray (I John 5:16). It is an "eternal sin" (Mark 3:29).

The "impossible" of Hebrews 6:4 does not mean that the soul has become too hard for the Holy Spirit to touch. The Holy Spirit is omnipotent and can do anything he wants. He can even take stones and make sons of God out of them (Matt. 3:9). But it is "impossible" because God no longer wills to convert the soul. This is just the punishment: God's abandoning the sinner to his own sins.

The judgment is similar to that recorded in Romans 1. Some, says Paul, clearly knew God; yet they did not glorify him as God, neither gave him thanks, but they suppressed this knowledge, became empty and dark-headed, and converted the glory of the incorruptible God into the image of corruptible man, birds, and animals (Rom. 1:18-23). Their punishment was the absence of God in their hearts, their abandonment to their own desires and passions, and their being given up to a reprobate mind (Rom. 1:24-32). Since man is so rotten morally, to leave him to his own likes is to guarantee that he will never be converted. This is precisely the kind of punishment that God metes out to those who have blasphemed against the Holy Spirit.

The punishment may be compared to a farmer's treatment of barren soil. If a piece of soil, after it has received much rain, produces no good crops but only thorns and thistles, then it is deemed worthless, is rejected, and is fit to be thoroughly burned. So also, if a man produces no faith and good works after he has been blessed with the powerful presence and work of the Holy Spirit, then he, too, is without value, is rejected and is fit to be thoroughly burned in the fires of hell (Heb. 6:7, 8).

If, after reading about this "fearful" (Heb. 10:27) punishment, someone trembles for fear that he has committed this sin and he desires to be saved, he should rest assured that he is not eternally lost. In the first place, if anyone asks the God-man Jesus Christ to save him, he may be absolutely sure that Jesus will accept him, for Jesus said, "Whoever comes to me I will never drive away" (John 6:37). God will accept graciously anyone who comes to him in faith, regardless of how heinous his sins may have been. This is the grand message of the Bible.

Secondly, the very essence of the unpardonable sin is that the sinner does not care to be saved. He hates Christ, and the last thing that is going to bother him is the question whether he did something wrong or not. God has given such a person up to his own wants and desires, which, without the Spirit's influences, are always away from and not towards God. Godly trembling is not possible with such a person. If anyone is now trembling, then that very anxiety is a sign of the working of the Spirit in his life. For without the Spirit no one would fear or care or want to be saved.

Although some reader may not have committed the unpardonable sin, there is the distinct possibility of his committing it in the future. The Hebrews had not committed the sin either. Thus the author says immediately following this section on the blasphemy against the Holy Spirit that he was persuaded of better things concerning them (6:9). But he did write an urgent warning to them, for there was a danger that they would fall into that grievous error.

They had heard the gospel of salvation but had not applied it to themselves as they should have. By the time the Epistle was written they should have been teachers. But instead they were still sitting in the pews and had to be taught "the elementary truths" of the Bible. They could only drink milk, not chew meat. They had become tired and sluggish in learning. Therefore, the author warned them that although he was persuaded of better things of them, there was a real danger that they could apostatize. There was a possibility that some, having heard the gospel so plainly and even having been moved by the Spirit so that they had tasted that the Word of God was good, would fall away. If they did, they could never return to God and be saved.

The obvious remedy for anyone who fears that he might fall into such a state is to turn now to Christ. He should never postpone such action, for that is part of the very nature of this sin—that those who know better postpone their decision until a more convenient time (Acts 24:25). Instead of putting off this decision, one who is truly concerned about not committing the unpardonable sin should make sure that he looks to the only Savior, the God-man Jesus, to save him. Secondly, he should study the Word of God so that he will advance beyond the elementary teachings about Christ, the milk of the Word (Heb.

5:12; 6:1). Their failure to study and grow in the Word of God was the primary reason the author was worried about the Hebrews. Obviously, the chief remedy for the Hebrews was to spend more time with the Holy Scriptures. For us that means such things as reading the Bible daily, using Biblical aids such as cross references and commentaries, going to church regularly, memorizing verses, attending Bible study groups, and discussing the Word. When a person turns to Christ and studies his Word, he may know that he is a child of God, saved by Jesus, and will never be lost.

The Holy Spirit and Human Responsibility 16

In the course of the foregoing chapters, we have seen how far-reaching are the works of the Holy Spirit. Great and varied is the realm in which the Spirit works. It is impossible to confine his activity to sanctification alone. The purpose of this book, however, is not that we may satisfy our idle curiosity about relatively unknown facts, but rather, that by having a more precise knowledge of the Spirit, we may be led to expect and experience more blessings from him. If we are to be Spirit-filled, we must know more of the Spirit and his work. But we must have more than knowledge; we must also do something. In this chapter we will see what our responsibility is in relation to the Holy Spirit. Let us first notice the realm in which there is no human responsibility, and then the realm in which there is.

I. Where There Is No Human Responsibility

If we were not on our guard, we might possibly represent regeneration as an act that man controls—as his responsibility. We might possibly quote Jesus' statement, "You must be born

187

again" (John 3:7), and then exhort: "In order to enter the kingdom of heaven you must be born of the Spirit. See to it, then, that you fulfill the necessary prerequisites of conviction, repentance, conversion, and faith in order that you may be regenerated. It is in your hands. Don't put it off, for you must be born again."

But such a representation would not be Scriptural. The Bible holds all men accountable for *all* of their actions, but not for the act of the Spirit in regeneration. Unregenerated man, even though dead in his sins and unable to do any spiritual good, is still responsible before God for his fall in Adam and all the resulting sin. He cannot escape guilt by thrusting the blame back on Adam. It is man's own fault that he is in such a moral predicament. Regenerated man, too, is responsible to God for all of his actions, whether it be his thinking or speaking or acting. But no man is responsible for the work of regeneration. It is not man's act. He does not beget himself, but as Jesus told Nicodemus, man is born from above, by the Spirit. Regeneration is solely the activity of the Spirit, and man is utterly passive in it, as we saw more fully in chapter 7.

Nor may we say that man is responsible for setting in motion that chain of events—that is, conviction, repentance, conversion, and faith in Christ—that will produce regeneration. For as we have seen, these events do not precede and cause faith, but as in the case of Lydia, regeneration must first occur in order that the lost may repent and believe.

It is noteworthy that nowhere in the Bible do we find a command for a man to be born again or for him to begin a process that leads to regeneration. When Jesus says to Nicodemus, "You must be born again," he does not command him to do so. Rather, he is simply stating a fact. It was necessary for Nicodemus to be born again if he was to enter the kingdom of heaven. He had to be born of water and the Spirit, that is, he had to be cleansed by the washing of regeneration, in order to enter in. Jesus does not tell Nicodemus that he is able to regenerate himself or that he must first do certain things in order to be regenerated. On the contrary, he strongly intimates that regeneration is not in his control at all. Rather, this birth is from above. Furthermore, says Jesus, the Spirit who begets is like the wind that blows wherever it pleases. No one controls it or dictates to it. Just as no one can fulfill certain conditions which would cause the wind to change its direction, neither can anyone, by fulfilling certain conditions, dictate to the Holy Spirit where he should regenerate.

Similarly, to use the Biblical illustrations of birth and resurrection, any commandment to man concerning regeneration would be like trying to ask a baby not yet born to comply with certain prerequisites in order that it might be born. Or it would be like asking dead Lazarus to perform certain obligations in order that Jesus might resurrect him.

Since, then, regeneration is an act that only the Holy Spirit can and does perform, and since the Bible tells us that man does not have to fulfill and indeed cannot fulfill certain conditions which obligate the Spirit to regenerate, the necessary conclusion is that man is not and cannot be responsible for regeneration, but that it is entirely in God's hands.

Although the Bible does not make man responsible for regeneration, it does place the responsibility of believing 100 percent on his shoulders. Nowhere does the Bible order man to be regenerated. But everywhere it exhorts him to believe. Regeneration belongs to the Holy Spirit, but faith belongs to man (even though it is the Spirit who enables him to believe). This Biblical emphasis must be our guide in witnessing and preaching to the unsaved. On the one hand, we must refrain from commanding them to be born again—that is *not* their responsibility; on the other hand, we must in the name of the King exhort, command, and beseech them to believe—that *is* their responsibility.

A word of caution must be interjected here. We should not distort the Biblical teaching that man is not responsible for his regeneration by inferring that the Bible teaches a fatalistic system of salvation. We might reason: If man cannot believe until he is regenerated by the Spirit of God, then it is not his obligation or responsibility to believe. But this is man's reasoning. We have to remain with the revelation of Scripture, even if its teachings go against our human reasoning. God's wisdom and knowledge are infinitely higher than ours, and we must submit to them even where they seem to defy human logic. Therefore, although the Bible teaches that regeneration precedes faith, and that regeneration is the sovereign choice of God and not the responsibility of man, yet, on the other hand, the Bible places all the responsibility upon man to believe. If he does not believe, it is *all* his fault, and not God's at all. If he does believe, all the praise belongs to God and none to man. *Soli Deo gloria:* Glory to God alone.[1]

II. Where There Is Human Responsibility

The Bible teaches us that after regeneration the Spirit lives in us in a special way. He possesses our souls and bodies. We are said to be temples of the Holy Spirit. There is a radical difference between ourselves and the non-Christian.

But the Scripture also intimates that there can be different degrees in the indwelling of the Spirit. He dwells more fully in one than in another. There can be a minimal possession or an abundant overflowing.[2] The disciples at Antioch "were filled with joy and with the Holy Spirit" (Acts 13:52). Paul commands the Ephesians, who already had the Spirit and Christ in their hearts, to be filled with the Spirit, and not with wine (Eph. 5:18). Instead of being exhilarated by debasing drunkenness, they should be exhilarated by the Holy Spirit. Then they will be "mature" men (Eph. 4:13), "thoroughly equipped for every good work" (II Tim. 3:17).

Thus there is a difference between merely having the Holy Spirit and being filled with the Holy Spirit. It is possible to have the Spirit to such an extent that he pervades every faculty, and yet to receive still more of him. We may have a new principle of life within us, such as the Holy Spirit, who changes our whole being and yet has not taken over to such an extent that he fills us to overflowing. Death has been dispelled and life is here, but it can be a sickly life that is corrupted with disease. There can be light, and yet it is only a dawn, and not noonday brightness. Likewise, we can have the Spirit within us so that our spiritual

---

[2] Some do not like to speak of "degrees" of the Spirit's indwelling, or of "an increased indwelling," or of "having the Spirit in all his fullness," reasoning that the Holy Spirit is either in you or not. Of course, what is meant by this Pauline expression of being "filled with the Spirit" (Eph. 5:18) is not that the individual receives, as it were, more of the Spirit in some quantitative way, but that the Spirit becomes more active in him. The Holy Spirit dwells in all Christians, all who are regenerated. But as he becomes more active, he increasingly sanctifies them. It is this activity or work of the Spirit that is meant by the expression "an increased indwelling of the Holy Spirit."

[1] For a fuller discussion of this problem, see the last chapter in the author's *The Five Points of Calvinism* (Baker Book House, 1972).

life is entirely different from our former spiritual death, but yet not so that we have him in all of his fullness.

As we have seen in a previous chapter, the secret of holy living is tied up inseparably with this indwelling of the Spirit of God. Without him it is impossible to do any good at all. But by the indwelling Spirit we can gain increasing victory over the power of sin in our lives. He gives to us a source of power that natural man does not have. He is the eternal fountain that springs up to everlasting life. After a person has become a Christian, the greatest goal of his life is to be completely filled with the Spirit.

Now that we have seen something of the different degrees in which the Spirit may indwell a Christian, the question is raised: Is there anything that we can do to possess a rich, full indwelling of the Spirit in order that we may be mature men of God, thoroughly equipped for every good work? Or must we simply wait until God moves us? In other words: Is man responsible for this fuller indwelling, or not?

In answer to this there are two pitfalls to be avoided. One is that view which holds that since everything, including even a fuller indwelling of the Spirit, has been foreordained by God, man can do nothing about increasing the indwelling of the Spirit and has no responsibility in this matter. Therefore, man should not even strive to receive a fuller indwelling, for everything will come to pass regardless of whether he tries or not. This passivist view, which teaches that man can do nothing and which leaves all in the hands of the Spirit, is unbiblical.

The other pitfall to be avoided is the opposite extreme: the activist viewpoint. It teaches that God has no final control over the increased indwelling of the Spirit, but that all of the responsibility rests on man. This view holds that man can frustrate the Spirit's purposes by resisting him. Therefore, man must allow the Spirit to work, or he will not work at all. Man, and not God, has the reins in his hands. This view, too, is unbiblical.

The Biblical solution, of course, lies in neither of these extremes, but rather in a balance of the two. And we do not mean a balance by which the Spirit does half the work and man the other half—a fifty-fifty proposition. Rather, it is a balance in which the Spirit is completely sovereign and man is completely responsible: a hundred-hundred proposition, as contradictory as that may seem. As in regeneration, so also in sanctification the Spirit has his irresistible purposes, and he accomplishes exactly what he desires. In this realm he is like the wind that blows where it pleases. But at the same time, although man is not responsible for the work of the Spirit in his new birth—in regeneration—he is completely responsible in relation to the later, sanctifying work of the third Person of the Trinity.

The first thing that should be noted about man's responsibility toward an increased indwelling of the Spirit is that God has given him means by which he may strive for that goal. One such means is faith. By intensely desiring and earnestly praying for sanctification and the indwelling Christ and Holy Spirit, and by confidently and firmly expecting that God will answer his prayer, he will receive a fuller reigning of Christ and the Spirit in his life.

All of the blessings of Christianity come to us by the means of faith alone. We are justified by faith in Christ as our Savior from the guilt of our sins. And no less are we sanctified by faith in Christ as our Savior from the power of our sins. We do not begin in faith only to be perfected by the law (Gal. 3:1-5). But the genius of the Bible—as historic Protestantism has correctly seen it—is that every spiritual blessing is obtained by faith alone. Christ is not only our redemption but also our sanctification (I Cor. 1:30). He revealed to Paul on the Damascus road that the saints "are sanctified by faith in me" (Acts 26:18).

Likewise, a fuller indwelling of the Spirit of sanctification is not received by works but by faith. We know from Galatians 3:14 that Christ was cursed for us, "that *by faith* we might receive the promise of the Spirit." In John 7:38, 39 we read: " 'Whoever *believes* in me, as the Scripture has said, streams of living water will flow from within him.' By this he meant the Spirit." Thus there is a direct relationship between faith and the indwelling Spirit. The greater our trust, the greater will be the indwelling of the Spirit and the consequent sanctification.

Furthermore, we know that the three Persons of the Trinity are inseparable, even in the matter of their living within Christians. Wherever the Spirit of Christ is, there is Christ himself (Rom. 8:9). And wherever Christ makes his home, the Father makes his, too (John 14:23). Because of this inseparability, all three come and live in the believer's heart by the same means. Since we know that it is by faith that Christ lives in us more abundantly, that means that the Holy Spirit does, too.

That Christ lives in us more richly by faith is seen from Ephesians 3:17, where Paul prayed for the Ephesians that Christ might live in their hearts through faith. That indwelling was not for the purpose of regeneration, because the Ephesians to whom Paul wrote were already regenerated and already had Christ living in their hearts. They were, after all, "the *saints* in Ephesus, the *faithful in Christ Jesus*" (1:1). Yet Paul prays that Christ may live in them by faith. The necessary inference is that faith is the means by which Christ comes into our lives more abundantly after regeneration. If that is true, then, because of the inseparability of the Persons of the Trinity, the Spirit comes into our lives more fully by faith, too. If we can increase the indwelling of Christ by faith, then we can increase the indwelling of the Spirit in the same way. For where Christ is, there is the Spirit also.

Another condition for the increased indwelling of God is to be found in Jesus' words: "If anyone loves me, he will obey my teaching. My Father will love him, and we will come to him and make our home with him" (John 14:23). He mentions the first condition, namely, love for himself, which, of course, includes faith. But a second condition, or, perhaps, just an outworking of the first, is obedience, that is, doing his will and being holy. In other words, if, after regeneration, we continue to believe and do not live in sin, then Christ and the Father, and by implication the Holy Spirit, will make their home in us more fully. Thus the fuller indwelling of the Spirit depends in part on our faith and our holiness.

Not only are faith and holiness necessary in order to have an increased indwelling of the Spirit, but, conversely, his work will be diminished by acts of rebellion on our part. That is implied by Jesus when he says that if a man loves him and keeps his word, he and the Father will make their home in him. In other words, if a man does not keep his word, but sins, they will not live in him.

Furthermore, Paul says, "Do not put out the Spirit's fire" (I Thess. 5:19). He is not referring only to the special gifts of the Spirit, such as the gifts of miracles, tongues, or prophesying, mentioned in the following verse. But this probably has reference to the more general work of the Spirit in his sanctifying operations. It must be remembered that it is impossible to quench the Spirit entirely, for, once saved, always saved. Yet it is possible to throw water on the Spirit of fire by sinning constantly and by failing to repent, believe, and stir up those sparks of life that the Holy Spirit has given us. We can thereby grieve him, taking joy away from him (Eph. 4:30; Isa. 63:10). This is anthropomorphic language, a speaking about God after the manner of men. But it indicates that the Spirit can be grieved and provoked, with the result that his influences are not so great upon us, and the union that we have with the Spirit is not as strong as it should be.

It can work both ways. We can increase the indwelling of the Spirit by faith and holiness, but we can also hinder his indwelling by a lack of faith and by sin.

This, then, is our responsibility toward the Holy Spirit. God has ordained that there should be a direct relationship between our faith and our holiness on the one hand, and the increased indwelling of the Holy Spirit on the other. The Spirit will dwell in our hearts in exact proportion to the faith that we have toward him. The more faith we have, the more the Spirit will come into our lives. We are not to be passive, as we must necessarily be in regeneration. Rather, God commands us to be very active. We must seek for a fuller indwelling of the Spirit. And if we fail to go to God and pray for the Holy Spirit, we shall not receive him in greater measure. For God has established the law that a fuller presence of the Spirit comes by faith. If we want holy living, then we must have the fountain of the rivers of life; and if we want the fountain—the supernatural source—then we must seek the Spirit by faith. That is the only way to victory.

Someone might ask: But is not this contrary to the foreordination by God of all things? Does not this make God dependent upon man, and the Spirit upon man's faith? The answer is: Of course not! God has foreordained the means as well as the end results.

For instance, the Bible teaches us that we will receive the Savior only by faith. If we reject Christ, we will not be saved. Salvation depends on faith in Christ. Similarly, as far as prayer is concerned, if we fail to pray for certain things, we will not, normally speaking, receive those things; and if we do pray for those matters according to the rules of prayer, we will receive them. The reason that these two facts do not contradict God's absolute foreordination of all things is that God has not only foreordained the end results, but he has also foreordained the means. He not only foreordains that a person should be saved, but also that he should believe in Christ. He not only foreordains certain events, but also that they should be prayed for.

So likewise, if we are to receive the fullness of the indwelling of the Spirit, we must also pray for that fullness. If we do not, we will not receive him more abundantly. The degree of the Spirit's living in us will depend on whether we seek him in faith or not. This is our responsibility. But, if we do pray for that Spirit and thereby receive him in a fuller measure, we must always remember that it was God who foreordained that we should pray for him, and that it was he who sent the Holy Spirit to cause us to pray. For, although we are to work out our own salvation with fear and trembling—although we may receive a greater measure of the Spirit by praying for him and by not grieving or antagonizing him—it is only because God is working in us to will and to do what pleases him that we do these very things (Phil. 2:12, 13).

This is the way God always works. He commands us to do great things, even impossibilities, and then he proceeds to give us the ability to fulfill what he commands us to do. He commands us, for example, to believe on Jesus Christ. But that is an impossibility for us in our natural state, and so we would say that we are unable to do so. But then God through regeneration gives us the ability to believe on Christ.

So also, God commands us to be filled with the Holy Spirit (Eph. 5:18). But this, too, is an impossibility for us in our own strength. God then gives us a greater working of the Spirit so that we can pray for an even greater measure of him. And because we pray for him, we do receive him even more fully. It is òur duty to strive for him with all that we have. But if we do, then it is only because the Spirit has already been working within us to pray and strive for him. God commands us and then enables us to do what he commands.

Thus, in determining man's responsibility in securing a richer indwelling of the Spirit, we see that the responsibility rests 100 percent on man. If he neglects the means that God has given, he will not have more of the Spirit. On the other hand, if he uses these means, he will have the Spirit in an increased measure. The obligation to seek this fuller indwelling of the Holy Spirit rests entirely with man.

At the same time, however, the work of giving the Spirit rests entirely with God—100 percent. This does not mean that man comes in his own native ability halfway to God and then God meets him and carries him the rest of the way—a fifty-fifty matter. No, God does it all. Man is 100 percent responsible, and yet God gives man *all* of the ability that he has. This is the gospel of grace—grace from the very beginning to the very end, and not halfway.

Now, admittedly, many of these things are hard to understand. They involve that great problem of relating divine sovereignty to human responsibility. For us it is impossible to reconcile them, although our infinite God can. All we can do is search them out as far as they are revealed in the Bible, and then leave the problem with God, resting on these two great truths that the Bible teaches us.

But this one thing we want to emphasize as we conclude: The Bible asserts unequivocally that faith and holiness produce a fuller indwelling of the Spirit. If we care little about being filled, if we do not seek it, if we yield to temptations, we will not have the Spirit of God in all of his fullness. But if we go to him and ask for him, he will come into our lives more fully. To be sure, God will enable us to do that; but, nevertheless, it is our fault if we do not. We are to blame. And it is to God's glory if we do. Therefore, let us put away sin, desire the Spirit, and ask for him in faith.

We may be assured that when we do that, we will certainly receive a fuller indwelling of the eternal Spirit of God. For which one of us, when our son asks us for a slice of bread, will give him a stone instead, or when he asks us for an egg, will give him a stinging scorpion? "If you then, though you are evil, know how to give good gifts to your children, how much more will your Father in heaven give the Holy Spirit to those who ask him!" (Luke 11:11-13). "Ask and it will be given to you; seek and you will find; knock and the door will be opened to you" (Luke 11:9). Pray for the Spirit, believe that you will receive him in greater abundance, and you will. If Christ is your Savior from sin, there can be no higher goal than this: to know the fullness of the indwelling of the eternal Spirit of God.